Why Me, Why Here?
Please, Some Answers

Best wishes

Grant Sanders

Why Me, Why Here?
Please, Some Answers

GGJ Sanders

First published in Great Britain in 2016 by Grant Sanders

ISBN 978-0-9934454-0-8

Printed by Biddles Books
www.biddles.co.uk

Prologue

The author would describe himself as an ordinary man who has had some extraordinary experiences. He has endeavoured to articulate these experiences and what he has subsequently learnt within the pages of this book. He is not a health professional, counsellor, guru or advisor of any kind and accepts no liability for how the information in this book is interpreted.

Dedication

This book is dedicated to Mick Vaughan 1968-2006 and the memories he left behind. Mick was a loving father, son, brother, uncle and my best friend. I could not have written this book without a visit from him on 12/10/2006, this visit began my journey to start questioning absolutely everything.

Contents

Introduction

Life, for me, is like a series of chess moves;
everything requires rational thought.
It's never wise to fumble through the game,
largely ignoring intricate detail and
still claim you know all the answers.

G.G.J.Sanders

Life has many experiences to offer us, not all of them are wonderful and not all of them can be easily explained. Some of us experience things that others have not; this may be for a variety of reasons. One of these could be due to geographical location, another may just be related to the age of the person who has had the experience. After all, I think we could agree the correlation that the older you get the more you experience.

There has been a study which highlights this point of view. In the vast mountain range of The Himalayas, which stretches hundreds of miles and crosses various different countries, there have been numerous sightings by many native adults.

Historically, there have been reports of individuals seeing a fierce creature standing on two feet with a pale looking face many feet taller than a human being. From then on it had a name which varied from the country around The Himalayas it had been witnessed, I will refer to it as 'The Yeti.'

The local people were terrified of this creature and so had a genuine respect for the danger it represented. So imagine some individuals weighing into the argument that put forward a theme of hallucination; the point of view that the sightings would occur at an altitude many thousands of feet above sea level and therefore people's minds were playing tricks with them. In a nutshell, they were suggesting that these individuals could not be relied upon to observe what was happening in front of their very eyes.

I like to call this theory of hallucination 'a throwaway theory' because it is so much easier just to dismiss something or someone as irrelevant and turn your back on them rather than conduct your own research and then come to a more logical conclusion. After all, in my view, human kindness and respect at the forefront of a search or investigation often goes a long way to unlocking doors.

Scientists decided to press on, roll up their sleeves and actually obtained hair samples that were left by this creature. As science readapts itself and grows from the knowledge already established a DNA profile would be examined from the core of the hair samples obtained from this creature. A few decades ago this technology was simply not in place.

Two workable samples were obtained that originated from two separate countries and the team did an analysis on them. The initial findings that came through DNA testing established that this creature was a match to a polar bear but with an added twist. It was not what we would deem a modern polar bear but an ancient polar bear that was thought to have died out thousands of years ago.

I have brought up this topic to highlight the point that we, as human beings, often want to pigeonhole things (and each other) quickly and move on but if we do that we often miss something. That potential truth is there lurking beneath the surface. All we need to do is dig a little; make that effort that some refuse to do. After all, the quicker we come to a conclusion about something, the more chance we realistically have of getting it completely wrong. Who hasn't been guilty of this? Those native to The Himalayas had indeed been correct after all. There was no hallucination and any eye tests booked on their behalf could now be cancelled.

Life has a habit of throwing obstacles into your path. This obstacle could be the possibility of changing job, moving to a different area or losing someone you care deeply about. Then a new path opens up before us and it is with a certain amount of trepidation that we take the first step and move down that new path and get to see what the future offers us.

My reason for writing this book is that I had a life-changing experience some years ago. This life-changing experience could not be described as 'the norm,' but it happened. Like those native to The Himalayas, I knew that this had happened, even though the enormity of the event was very puzzling to me. I then realised that I needed to get answers to the multitude of questions that were popping into my head. I wanted my answers.

Indeed after completely opening up, like those scientists, I believe I have them. This gap between the event and the first publication of this book represents many years of knowledge growth and many years of reflection. I must clarify here that this book has not been written on a whim. I can still recall the incident like it was yesterday. I will go on to explain it fully in chapter five.

Now, I want to stand up, be counted and lay my hand on the table for all to see but I can only do this by telling my story and unravelling things piece by piece, an open book approach to my life and the findings that followed. I hope in the chapters that follow, particularly those of you who have ventured down a new path with trepidation, will see that I recall events through honesty and integrity.

One thing that you must know about me at this point is that I have always been interested in facts and not fantasy. I would rather pick up a factual book rather than anything related to fiction, but I am sure there will be some who would want to pigeonhole my journey as the latter. This, of course, is upsetting, but I realise it is part of life; criticism is often only just around the corner.

I do, however, have my very own photographic evidence that I show interested friends and acquaintances and just for the record I would agree to sit a polygraph test in the future under the correct conditions to back-up any experience that has happened in my immediate environment.

There have been many times that I have wrestled with my inner thoughts on whether to keep these findings limited to people I know and come across in my future or set them free and let them work for others. I have decided on the latter and if I truly help even a small number of individuals move forward with a life that currently makes little sense, but they know they need more answers, I hope I have helped with this book. My early message to you, the reader, is to be true to yourself through adversity. After all, you know who you are when others may offer nothing of themselves but harsh words and critical judgements.

So I urge you to read on not only with an open mind but also with an open and trusting heart so that I can share these lessons learnt and I leave you to reflect on the content and move forward in your own unique way. I have been as descriptive as I possibly can about these things that have happened in my immediate environment that will be revealed within the coming pages.

Chapter 1

Observing others

Sometimes we have to observe how other people react to us. They may know us, they may not, but we can usually gauge by their body language whether they're impressed or not that we occupy the same surroundings.

There's that person, behind you, at the supermarket that almost takes your heel off with their trolley and then slaps every item on the conveyor belt. The person that moves across your vehicle at the junction with their car then sits still making the 'T' shape rather than let you pull out and join the traffic.

Then there's the parent that puts half of their pushchair into the path of your moving vehicle so they can cross the road now, using their own child as a human stop sign, rather than wait for a safe space. The parent that gets their child into the back of their car on the road in the way of oncoming traffic rather than just being on the path, hitching the child along to their seat.

We could all make a list of things we find mildly disturbing about the thought processes of others and who's to say that one of my idiosyncrasies wouldn't be in your list or someone else's if compiled here and now. My reason for highlighting parents is that I seriously love children and if I change one person's way of thinking, already this early in the book, I could at least help to prevent an accident. Going back to my last point, it is never good seeing a child near the middle of the road and if you have ever gone across a roundabout in your car and then tried to remember actually doing it, when your head is full of the stresses of life, this highlights the point.

I am confident that by the end of this book a strong feel of these issues will prevail and indeed the much bigger ones yet to come that form part of the big picture. Not forgetting there is enough information around us to continue to learn something else no matter what qualifications we have or the age we reach.

Firstly, let me set up a scenario. There is MR.A and MR.B, who are both young men around the early twenties age. MR.A is a bit of a livewire who loves to be out every night and will tell any male that will listen he has slept with dozens of women of all ages. His friends come and go and at the moment he feels there is no time for a job. There is simply too much fun to be had.

MR.A doesn't like being in the same place for long. He appears to get all his money from his parents but doesn't want to talk about it when approached because he feels that this is their job to provide for him. Deep down the feeling is that they brought him into this world and he had no choice in the matter, therefore they must continue to look out for him. However, he wouldn't speak of his thoughts just in case his lucrative arrangement changed.

MR.B by comparison is calm and responsible. He is currently employed and although it's not his ideal job he will give it his commitment. He is unassuming and polite; mainly speaking when he is spoken to. He appears to give out respect even though sometimes the respect coming back falls a little short. He is single and quite shy where the fairer sex is concerned. He longs for a woman that he can share his life with but remains unlucky in love.

When we meet someone for the first time we don't know much information about them. Without the information just stated, some would say MR.A was exciting and some would feel that MR.B was a little boring.

Now you know more about their personality, think about this for a short while. Who would you rather take care of your camera with all the great photos you have just taken? Who would you want to hold your wage packet while you get your coat? Who would you like to guard your drink at a social event whilst you visit the toilet? I think you would be able to guess my answer.

Throughout life, we are making decisions like this all the time and we find that our circle of friends builds up around the choices that we have made for ourselves in the duration we have been on this planet. Effectively we are choosing who we want to be associated with. After all, nobody forces me to make my own decisions.

This is where I start to put some meat on the bones as I actually knew and worked with MR.B, the latter of our two men.

MR.B, approximately five years older than me, worked with me when I had my first job as a teenager in a warehouse. It took us some time to get to know each other but, after we were familiar with each other, we had many conversations on our own in the wines and spirits section that he overlooked. We both liked sport, so that was always a conversation starter and, after a while, he called me cookie as a nickname. I'm not fully sure why but it may have been because I did an impression of the cookie monster.

After many months of knowing this guy, I found out that he had health problems that were not going to go away with time. This made me feel bad as I was blessed with good health.

One day, we were again alone in the wines and spirits section and after a few pleasantries he looked me in the eye. He said in a calm but very serious manner that a short while ago he had got out of bed in the middle of the night and, as he approached the door, he looked around to have one last look at the room, a mere glance, when he saw his own body still lying in his bed with closed eyes. He told me categorically that this was not a dream; there was no smile on his face and it wasn't April 1st.

What did I do when told this? The answer was that I immediately went cold and felt the hairs on my body standing to attention. I didn't exactly know what to say. We left things there for as a young man I was not a great conversationalist, especially of things that I didn't understand. My mindset has always been if you don't know much about a particular subject keep quiet, let others talk and you might learn something. A few seconds later we both turned around and got on with our work. Neither of us approached the subject again.

I'm sure virtually everyone, whether directly or indirectly will be aware of someone similar to MR.A used in this example. So let's examine things for a moment before moving on. Would I, as a young man, have accepted this story from MR.A? Honestly, no, I wouldn't but a guy I knew and respected had told me this after many months of knowing him. I feel he had reached out to me at a soul level.

In situations like this, with wisdom now on my side, it should come down to one word and that is 'trust.' Did I trust him? Yes, I did. Did I believe him? The answer was yes, but I didn't fully understand his story when he relayed it to me at that time.

I did feel he had confided in the right person, without a doubt. I have never been a person for rushing over to someone else and having a gossip, pointing fingers when someone has confided in me. I kept it to myself, for reasons of my respect for him. In fact, the only other person I have ever told up to now is my wife.

Over the next few months of being told this I spent a lot of time thinking about what he had said and doing some metaphorical head scratching. At that time, I was living with my mother, stepfather and many siblings in an old farm house. I was living in a different part of the house to everyone else and my room felt a little dark and spooky.

I know for a fact that when I got out of bed I would have muttered to myself under my breath about not seeing anything behind me. After all, I always checked my walk in wardrobe was empty before I went to bed so that I could sleep soundly. It's just the way I'm wired. I believe it could be some sort of fight or flight mechanism that people always seem to be talking about. That and I once caught my mother hiding in there to frighten the living daylights out of me one day after I had returned from College.

Chapter 2

The man who.........
didn't realise what
was coming

I have heard it said that there are two types of people, those that have lost someone and those that have yet to lose someone.

When you are approaching your late twenties you are very fortunate if you have not experienced losing someone that is very close to you. This is how my life had initiated. I hadn't lost a family member that meant the world to me, I was lucky. Of my four grandparents, one had died before I was born but the other three were still around.

My wife soon conceived and I was to be a father for the second time; then came the passing of four people that had formed part of my life, within three years of each other. These were, all of my remaining grandparents and also my much-loved father-in-law who was called Roy. In fact, Roy was the first, one year after my son made his appearance into this world. Roy could have been described as a family man of the highest calibre, he simply never stopped giving of himself and I held him in the highest regard. Often the good ones don't sing their own praises and that was the mark of the man I knew.

My wife was distraught and it took a lot to get through the funeral. Also, she was very saddened because it was decided that her father was not going to be buried but cremated. She wanted a grave with a headstone to attend to, but her wishes were overlooked.

In reality, she had a little patch of ground to visit at the crematorium but she could not locate this exact patch because of her mother's wishes regarding the ashes being scattered above ground. This led to a lot of frustration on my wife's part. How could she grieve properly when everything seemed so impersonal? For her, it was impossible. A huge void seemed to appear instead of that warm, loving man that seemed to spend his whole life providing with a smile. A reserved man that didn't utter the words of love to those around him but he showed them through his many actions.

Soon it was told that approaching the point of death, Roy suddenly looked at a part of the room that was seemingly empty and had a radiant smile on his face. He was not heavily sedated or to my knowledge on medication. My wife, considered his favourite, did not witness this last smile because he had held on until she came away from his house and I was at home looking after the children. However, it had been witnessed shortly before he slipped away. But why? He had a terminal illness. Surely you don't smile when you are in such pain and distress and what was he actually smiling at?

Soon came another bullet point in my life that I could not understand at this time. Sixteen months after Roy's passing (I keep a diary) my small son was in his grandfather's old front room when he pointed next to Roy's favourite chair in the corner of the room and said, "Man, granddad." It was a heart-stopping moment that caused us all around the event to take a sharp intake of breath and stop what they were doing.

What had that two-year-old boy said? There were adults around him that saw absolutely nothing. Where did he get that from? There were not even any photographs up to satisfy us of a genuine misunderstanding.

Here, I feel that I should mention that Samuel was a very bright little boy. On a visit to the doctors, being only a few months old, we told the doctor that he said one word and that was 'drink' when he was hungry and wanted his milk. The doctor looked at us with a 'yeah right' expression and took him off us for his check-up. Then it came just as the doctor took hold, "Gink." The doctor's chin almost hit the floor.

A few months after the sighting, we decided that we should heed the evidence being presented to us and thought it might be time to see a medium, someone that could provide a link between us and the spirit world (if there was one.) After all, if a loved one had died and you wanted to communicate, this was the only way forward. For us, it was either this or nothing. The fear of nothing for the rest of my wife's life would lead to hopelessness, it wasn't even an option.

One was recommended to us by a third party, which is a fantastic start, word of mouth. So we travelled a fair few miles and saw a middle aged lady and I remember the content of the sitting, it went well.

She established a link with an elder man whose personality sounded exactly like Roy with no information coming from us. She often paused like she was listening to someone speaking, which I later discovered had a term 'clairaudience,' then she asked us if we had a small son which was confirmed. Then a blow like a professional boxer delivers "Does he point out to the corner of the room and say 'man' in this man's old house?"

A shiver came over us. This fact was never uttered to anyone outside the family. There we were talking to a woman that knew absolutely nothing about us and she was revealing this information. My respect for mediumship had just taken a massive leap forward, but my understanding at that time needed to catch up.

Now let me explain about my mindset at this time. Of course, I was a family man that wanted to help provide for his own family but also, I must have been a little cynical about the things I didn't understand or care to understand.

Then I found no enjoyment in reading whatsoever, which in reflection was a bad start. I was typically the sporty type that hated sitting still too long because I got twitchy. In fact, the only time I was put under pressure to read books was during my last two years at secondary school when we had to read twelve books in two years. Every book you read had to have a book report to give your views on the book content. Although I feel I have good writing skills, if I could have given up English at this point I would have. As a teenage boy, this filled me with dread. At the end of that second year, all the students, mainly boys, who hadn't read the twelve books started to panic and I don't mind telling you that I was one of them.

I was very scared of death, after all, you were so vibrant and had this personality and zest for life and all of a sudden nothing. The life had gone, you drift into nothingness and await a possible post mortem. All that you had ever learnt was gone and nobody could benefit from any talents that you once had. I had always scratched my head and wondered why we say great things about people who have died and yet we never collectively seem to address that person with positive comments of warmth and tenderness when they are actually alive.

These were my views. Also, what if you did feel pain, yet nobody but you knew as you lay there with closed eyes and no expression? I tried not to think about it, but it would eventually catch up with me during daily activity, like waiting for the kettle to boil or getting the washing from the line, and my smile that was always part of me would slowly disappear.

At this period of my life, I felt very uncomfortable about the word 'God.' There was a vicar that lived opposite our old family home (already mentioned) and one day he was talking to my mother and commented that his adult son had recently changed his views about God and now saw the light. Although he was very impressed with this, I was not, and found no comfort in the conversation, choosing to distance myself from it.

When I saw various sporting athletes look up to the sky and cross their chest after a race I would roll my eyes with disapproval. Why on earth would they do such a thing? After all, who were they looking at and gesturing to? There was no one there. I remembered on one occasion in my life a Christian had come to my property and wanted to come in and talk about God. She had caught me on the hop so I told her that I was an atheist and she soon scurried away. It seemed the easiest way to end a conversation that you didn't want to be part of.

I thought that I was a realist. We had five senses and nothing more. Surely nothing that you cannot touch, smell, see, hear or taste truly exists. Nobody that I knew and respected had ever told me anything to the contrary or something that I could not understand. The only exception was that day in the warehouse with MrB. To believe anything different to this required faith and I didn't have any of that.

Up to that point, I was always hearing people saying that you only live once and the only guarantees in life were death and taxes. I was influenced by this without probably realising. On a subconscious level it became part of my thinking, the more I heard these and many other sayings the more influence it had. After all, if the majority of people had similar views, then surely I was in the winning team.

Back to my little boy's comment and the visit to see this medium, I now had a problem and I could not get this out of my mind. A complete stranger had now told me information that shook my previous views to their core.

If I was to maintain my previous views on life and death there was a barrier in the way. I had always viewed myself as a thinker whether that sounds appropriate or not at this stage. I was beating adult members of my extended family at chess as a young teenager, after all. I do not like overlooking a fact that gets into my path and say, "Oh well we will just let that slip." The enlightened thinkers of the world just don't do that. If I had done this in the warehouse that day when I was a teenager, it wasn't going to happen again. I felt myself being more open to what life had to offer me and less pessimistic.

The thinking part of me was very evident as a young lad, it now just needed fresh material injected into it to re-stimulate. Indeed, I once asked my mother about child birth one day as a small boy; this has since been relayed to me several times. I asked her if I came from her tummy and she replied that I had. Then I put my finger in the air and said to her, "Therefore you and me must have been in your mummy's tummy together at some point." Think about that one from a child.

Chapter 3

The vivid dream lays the foundations

Disbelieving in something that you cannot grasp
with your five senses is more of a state of mind
than a stroke of genius.

G.G.J.Sanders

When my grandmother died, who was my maternal grandmother, it was quite expected as she was in her eighties and had lung cancer, smoking all her adult life. She had never remarried after my grandfather died before my birth.

There had always been a strong link between us, unlike the grandparents on the paternal side, who acted like I had never existed after my mother divorced my father when I was around five-years- old. It was as though they used a young child as a scapegoat to get their revenge on my mother. There were to be no birthday cards, no Christmas cards, no visits, in fact, nothing. Indeed, I had to go to their house through my father later on in life (now that's forgiveness) to see them. They eventually even declined an invitation for my wedding day.

My maternal grandmother, on the other hand, was the one who looked after me as a child at the drop of a hat with no questions asked. She was the one that would give you her last five-pound note no matter how much you said that you didn't want it. As her first grandson making observations, the only people that I ever remember entering her house were family or people that she knew inside out.

When I was a young boy I had to have a physical examination at school, where all the boys lined up and approached two old ladies. Depending upon which lady you found yourself in front of she would cup her hand around your bare genitals and either nodded okay or shook her head. There were no screens and no privacy. It was a humiliating experience that was like a human production line, but it was my much-loved grandmother alone who stood beside me during this horrible experience.

I remember my grandmother's concerned face for me, but we never seem to question enough. Someone somewhere has made a decision good or bad and we just play along with it, it's out of our control. If we object we unsettle the apple cart and draw unwanted attention and then everyone looks in our direction. Best just go with the flow and keep your head down. This must be a

23

thought that in all honesty has happened not only to me but countless others I dare say too.

I was a shy boy and felt uncomfortable kissing anybody but giving her a kiss on the cheek always felt so natural. When she died I was living in a two bedroomed flat with my wife and two children of our own. We had had a tough time of things, but we were looking to finance a move.

The flat was amongst eleven other apartments. They were stacked three high, separated into two lots of six, so there were two main entry doors leading to the twelve apartments. It was a very noisy environment and respect seemed to be at a premium. Sometimes in life all you have to do is cross someone's path and they hate you just for being there. We had major problems with one of our neighbours in particular and it was during this experience I learnt one of my life's lessons.

If you are blighted by unreasonable behaviour then rely on your friends and family. Arrange family outings to more quiet places where you children can run and play. Soon things will change and it took nearly two years going through almost anything you can think of before we could finance a move to a modest three bedroom end terraced property in the adjacent county.

A few months after my loving grandmother died I had a vivid dream that involved her. In the dream, the two of us were in her old house that she died in. I was sitting at one side of the kitchen table with my back to the external entrance door. She was sitting looking into my eyes on the other side and we were holding hands across the table. In the dream, I knew that she had died, but I felt no reason at all to be scared. Why would I be scared you ask? Well after all I was holding hands with a deceased person; this to me seemed quite alarming when I woke up.

As she had looked into my eyes in this dream she told me that I must not worry about her now, she was safe and okay now in her new life where she was and then said something that sounded odd. She told me that she no longer needed to eat or drink anything because she obtained her energy from other means. This comment sounded so very strange, but with time and under-standing I was to find that it would make the hairs on the back of my neck stand to attention.

I have to say at this point that my maternal grandmother had a very distinct smell that went with her in life. Obviously, she smoked but the smell everyone remembered was that when she reached for her cigarettes or last five-pound note there was that distinct smell of her Halls menthol cough sweets that escaped from her handbag when the zip opened. We had so many games of cards as grandchildren in her company and always that smell would permeate the environment.

When we had moved into our new, quiet end terrace house my wife had the full-time job and I was the house husband. I worked part- time and did the school runs, cooking, washing and having the occasional cat nap on the settee too (if I'm honest.) I was often alone in the house and at this time we had not yet got our Jack Russell puppy but that was our plan.

On one particular day months after this dream, I was alone upstairs. All of a sudden, there was that smell that I remembered so well from my childhood in my bedroom. It was very powerful, like an explosion of scent. This had come out of the blue, that distinct smell of Halls menthol cough sweets. I didn't like them, my wife didn't eat sweets and the children in all honesty would have refused them even if they had been at home or we had a pack in the cupboard for them to suck.

At the time of this smell, I didn't know what to do but what can you do? I remember being totally confused and if I had seen my own face in the mirror at that moment it would have been contorted thinking about what had just happened. It was another experience around the family where there was evidence of a seemingly former member of the family who was very loving and caring but with no visible identity to them.

It was beginning to dawn on me that our senses work within ranges and it did not really matter which of our five senses it related to. If there was a radar, then we as humans simply don't have that complete range to work with, certain things were simply off limits to us outside of that rotating dial and therefore no blip showing on our metaphorical screen.

If we look at hearing, humans are able to hear sounds up to 20 kHz but the greater wax moth is believed to sense sound up to 300 kHz. Grizzly bears are also believed to have a sense of smell 100,000 times better than humans. So in a similar fashion are we to believe that our eyes are any different?

Addressing this from personal experience, we once had a fabric settee that we purchased new. Long before pets we found that during the course of its life we were being bitten by something that appeared to be invisible when we sat on it. A change to leather from fabric and the problem went away overnight never to return. My conclusion: dust mites, that we can't see, were biting us.

So if this is at one end of the scale where does the scale lead to? I for one do not see this scale as a graph that things can be simply plotted along it on an 'X' and 'Y' axis. For me it was a scale that had dimensions and therefore not one that could be arranged in a student's workbook, there was simply more to it than we can ever imagine.

We live in a physical world where, if a murder was thought to have been committed with no body available and evidence suggesting the person's finances had not been accessed, how could anyone prove it when the body was nowhere to be seen? It works in similar circumstances for the spirit world in the sense that there is no body for our limited senses to pick up, so how can we prove their existence?

The spirit world has yet to be categorically proven so many will be met with insults if their views are not among common thinking. It is my view that it has not been categorically proven because science and technology at this point of our existence and in the great scheme of things are simply not at the relevant level for it to be proven. I am thinking here that this comment may have drawn a gasp by one or two readers. Well we should perhaps try telling this to qualified pilots that have recorded seeing a UFO when in flight and it darting away from them at a speed close to infinity (with little audible sound) when it has plagued them for long enough.

In looking at the advances we have made as a society in the last fifty years, are we to presume that we are now finished and we are at the top of our game and in the next fifty years we can add little? I for one think that advances will keep coming at a steady rate if we remain free from worldwide conflict involving nuclear weapons.

If we look at the motor car alone it is now almost impossible for anyone to steal an up to date car without having the car keys. I believe in the next few decades, as technology moves through it's gears, it will be almost impossible for someone to drive without insurance or drive under the influence of alcohol or drugs.

In society I feel it generally works like this, an occurrence will be proven by science or technology and then the public will then begin to trust the facts and follow suit, like the story in my introduction. There always seems to be a period in our history when this has happened. When those thought that the world was flat Galileo stepped forward in around 200AD. He measured the angle of the sun from different geographical locations to prove otherwise.

More recently vast amounts of new planetary systems have been found, by the Kepler telescope, with similar earth type planets to ours that they believe can sustain life. In the distance is a star similar to our sun. Imagine those that thought this was hogwash until it was proven by advancing technology.

After the experience with my grandmother's fragrance, I later did my own search into this phenomenon and found that it already had its own terminology. It is regarded as a form of after death communication (ADC) by experts. It is actually called an 'olfactory ADC' and this and many other events like it happen to ordinary people just like you and me that grieve the loss of loved ones.

Before the next chapter, it is very important for me to state that we don't need a person beside us holding a clipboard and tick-sheet following us around 24/7 to verify our own experiences. Likewise, when you have a powerful experience you don't immediately need to look for the telephone and press speed dial to ask somebody's permission if you were allowed to have it. However, when you do have them you need a little courage because it is very hard not to speak out. For me, it is all about finding the correct person to converse with who has a sensitive nature.

When you do this you will get to know rather quickly that you are not alone. With experience, I am confident in saying that the vast majority of human beings, regarded as being a mature age, will have had an experience that they cannot explain using their five senses. Indeed, I could quite easily have created more chapters with all the stories related back to me (maybe my next book) from unassuming people; who at the back of their minds thought that their current view of reality was being tested.

Chapter 4

The can of worms
opens itself

Our new house that we were now in was everything that the flat was not. Things were very quiet during the day and night, it had an enclosed rear garden and the laughter came back to us as a family, that seemed to have been starved from us just weeks earlier. Also, our two children could escape their bunk beds and have a room each.

In everyday life, one of the things I do when I get ready to wash up is get the rubber gloves that are usually inside out from the last wash and blow into them. This causes them to turn the correct way, but the person coming past me at that time will get the full force of the water from them in their face. Then I have a laugh out loud moment when the member of my family lets out a shriek and reaches for a towel.

So imagine the irony when the laugh out loud moment is reversed and myself being the individual who had water on their face but with a twist, there was no visible identity of who had got me.

I was alone in our new home, as in the previous set of circumstances in the last chapter when all of a sudden I was splashed in the face with water. My heart skipped a beat, I was all set to rush to the stop cock and then phone the plumber. We had an emergency and water would be gushing through the ceiling at any moment. Then all of a sudden nothing, my face was still wet but everything went back to normal. There was no leak, no hysteria needed and the house was still empty apart from me.

Can you imagine telling someone this and not being laughed at? Well, I told my wife and within twelve months the same thing happened to her when we were in different rooms. The thing is my wife has always believed me without question. This has taken me longer to do myself and I have been addressing this and working hard on it. I don't want to fall into that category that always doubts, it's too easy an option because you are effectively giving nothing of yourself.

A classic example of this was when my wife came back from work one day and said that a guy on a green motorcycle had come past stationary traffic, with her in it, in a 30 MPH zone doing at least 80MPH and she had jumped out of her skin. My thoughts at that time were 'no way.'

I suggested that surely it wasn't that fast. I was soon to make myself look small when a few days later 'whoosh' that same guy came past me in similar circumstances on his green motorcycle. When I returned home I apologised straight away, again no clipboard and tick sheet scenario needed here.

Now the water incident was one of many occurrences that started to happen in the quietness of our new home. Our electrical appliances particularly our television was making noises like someone had whacked the back of it with the palm of their hand and I don't mean a tap. However, there was no actual movement, it's not as if the television wobbled.

This particular television was not faulty in any way. We had purchased it when our daughter was very young and we only parted with it in the end because digital television was making its intervention some fifteen years or so after we bought it. After all, this television had been with us in our time at the flat and nothing occurred. The only sound previous to this was coming from the speakers.

When sometimes I would stay up late on my own till the early hours of the morning and fall asleep, there would be that bolt of noise going through the television and I would wake up with a start realising that I should be tucked up in bed.

After this, our computer had noises of its very own but of a different calibre of sound, like someone picking up a little stone and firing it at the appliance with a catapult. This would happen frequently and I soon realised that if we were watching a particular game show on the television where the possible outcomes were A, B, C or D, the noise would correspond to the correct answer, whether the contestant was correct or not. I can tell you the general knowledge coming through was spot on and like an additional person in the room that couldn't be heard by voice getting their opinion across.

When you add to this other phenomena such as wooden chairs clicking as if someone living had just gotten up when in our reality there is nobody there. Then there is the sudden footstep on the upper part of the house when everybody is downstairs and your neighbours joined to you are away. You then start to question your own sanity but the whole family are going through this same experience, not just one person.

In the early hours one morning, I also visited the toilet at approximately 3AM to hear light, piano music weave through the house in a quiet and gentle manner. When I checked on everyone they were asleep and this has happened to me more than once. Our joined neighbours never play music and certainly don't have a piano.

––––––––––

If it isn't fight it must be flight

Then one day an event would happen to make everything previous to it seem like child's play.

By this time we had got our Jack Russell 'Monty' and I was alone in the house with him because our children were at school and my wife was at work. I went upstairs to visit the bathroom and told Monty that he had to wait downstairs, which he did.

I wasn't up there for long and as I came back to the top of the stairs and started to put one foot on the steps to come down, I glanced into the bathroom for one last time when I saw something move. My heart started to beat faster, a towel had moved upwards on its own like being levitated.

The towel was on a hook so that anyone could dry their hands on it. It then raised as if someone was drying their hands, maintained its new shape and position for around ten seconds, then laid to rest in the original position still on the hook. I looked on with a loose jaw.

I had just come out of the bathroom and I could see that nobody was there and a draught was not possible as the windows were closed. To reiterate, imagine someone wiping their hands on a towel, the towel goes up but is still attached to the hook, then the person is finished and lets the towel go. That's what happened. I saw it with my own eyes.

I took one last long look into the bathroom and saw Monty waiting for me at the bottom of the stairs. I then moved down them rather quickly and spent the next ten to fifteen minutes pacing up and down our back garden path reliving the events that had just happened, not wanting to revisit the house. I didn't smoke but if someone had offered me a cigarette at this point I would have taken it.

Eventually, I had enough courage to go back into my empty house and spent many minutes groping around with the towel to see if I could repeat the previous actions. You then come up with a word or phrase that best describes what has occurred and the most appropriate phrase at that time was 'a haunting.' 'That's it!' I thought. 'We have got a ghost, a spirit present.'

If you have an analytical mind as I felt that I did, you then start to do some research. After all, there are two sides to the coin, one is pretend nothing has happened like burying your head in the sand and the other is to question absolutely everything, which has now become my philosophy on life. Don't let anyone tell you what to think for fear of ridicule. You are an individual, don't ever suppress your thinking.

I found that our house was built in approximately 1972. It had been built on land that had been an apple orchard prior to the construction. The neighbours, who had all been around for some time, knew nobody who had died in the property. The people who had occupied the house before us were approaching middle age and had two children under ten-years-old. They had lived at this address for years.

I felt I had little to go on, but I was now completely open to different planes of existence. I could not come up with the sum total of what was with us at this point in time but knew that it existed in a different way to me and, as far as I knew, it meant us no harm. It's not as if it was coming into our bedrooms during the night to stop us getting the rest we all needed.

Chapter 5

The interacting shadow figure

I am but a drop in the ocean in this world of ours I meander this way and that way moving with the current going with the flow according to the pattern. However, every once in a while a SPLASH occurs that releases me to rise above and observe things from a greater vantage point. It is in these rare moments that I begin to see things more clearly and I develop a new perspective of my immediate surroundings. It is then and only then that I truly start to think like the sheepdog, rather than the sheep.

G.G.J.Sanders

I am sure that every loving parent will relive the births of their children and their wedding day. However, I'm not afraid to admit that the 12th of October 2006 is the day that I relive most of all. After all, it is a day that I had a life-changing experience. In fact, it rocked my soul to its very foundations. That day was a Thursday. Look it up if you like because I can't forget it, not even if I try.

My wife and myself have worked many jobs between us just to eke out a basic standard of living and it was my night to work in the garage as a cashier. In happier times, I had been a quantity surveyor and a manager of a care establishment but I was down on my luck again. However, a job is a job, and you have to give it your commitment. If you have ever been made redundant, try your very best to forgive those who have acted against you as, if you don't, it can be very consuming.

That night I had begun my responsibilities at 7PM. I was working with a female colleague who was around ten years or so my senior that I seemed to click with. If it was one thing about this job that I really liked, it was being separate from the supermarket we also represented. We were our own bosses in a way, separate and without any management around.

After thirty to forty minutes of my shift we were alone, just the two employees, seated and ready to serve anyone who approached us. The customers were all outside on the forecourt and none in front of us which was rare because we had one of the busiest garages in the area. My colleague was looking out towards the forecourt for what we called 'drive-offs' and I was looking towards the stock from my seated position, soon to get ready to put some more out.

All of a sudden, my attention was distracted towards my left-hand side as far away from the customer entrance as you could get. A dark shape had entered the room, a silhouette of a person. Shadow-like it came through the wall but for some reason it wasn't upright when it came through it. Imagine an adult climbing out from the bottom bunk of a set of bunk beds as this is how it came into the room. On the other side of this wall was our staff washroom. It was like a tear in the fabric of our reality had happened to let this shadow figure loose.

The image of this shadow was like holding the negative of a 35mm camera exposure up to the light and seeing a person dressed in dark colours. All you can see is darkness filling a human shape.

The shadow figure then stood upright as soon as it came through the wall and seemingly began to walk. It walked past my line of vision from left to right and I immediately thought 'whatever that was has gone and I don't need to bother with it anymore.' Wrong, it slowed up and then put itself into reverse crossing my line of vision for a second time; then a final very slight movement back to the right and it stood bolt upright in front of me as if looking at me face to face with recognition. I can only explain the stance of this figure as if it had unfinished business with me, it seemingly crossed my path more than once so that I had no way of missing this.

It was now standing approximately two feet in front of me. It was so close to me that I could just about touch it, or put my hand through it, whatever the case may be. The height of the figure was about five feet eight inches tall and seemed to have a male shape. Nobody else was in the environment, still me seated on the left, my colleague still seated on the right and the shadow figure standing in front of me.

It was as if time had slowed down, the customers were oblivious to everything. They were to the right of my colleague, still on the forecourt and still filling up their vehicles. The nearest customer was about thirty feet away through a window, standing and looking at his pump with his back to us.

The shadow figure appeared as if it was looking me up and down, but I did not notice the head move. It was so obvious that this figure was here for my attention alone, this cannot be overstated. Then, all of a sudden and without warning, like in a puff of smoke, it was gone and I was alone with my colleague once more.

I followed up with a howl of "Did you just see that?" to see my colleague turn to me with a blank expression and a shrug of the shoulders, "No," came the answer. She had been observing the forecourt all this time.

Soon everything was restored and the customers started to approach our entrance door one by one. I had to work the remainder of my shift thinking about what had happened. Although I continued to do my usual chores during that evening, everything that happened after this incident was a complete blur due to my concentration thinking about the event. I just have to hope that I gave the correct change or paperwork, as the case may be, to the customers.

I usually had any conversations with my wife the next morning because when I arrived home it was always close to 1 AM. To wake her up would be disrespectful as she had to be up early for her job. So, when we were both awake the next morning, I relayed the events to her that I had seen what was deemed as a ghost.

How do you convey to someone that you have seen a ghost and it actually tried to interact with you? Well, again there was a calm accepting response from her. She never doubted me, not even for a second. After all, there was a lot going on in our home that nobody could explain.

That morning, after my wife had gone off to her work, I sat with a cup of coffee trying to understand the events of the previous night at work. The shadow figure had come into my work area looking for me and had found me and stood in front of me, so there was no chance of a misunderstanding. But why had it happened? What did it want with me? I try my best to avoid confrontation in life and don't make a habit of trying to upset anyone. 'Just put your head down and get on with life,' has always been my motto.

I had worked this job for many years and it's not as if I was not familiar with my immediate surroundings. I soon decided that I didn't want to experience this again, especially if I were completely alone. I think I would have run off with my hands flapping in the air, just like my wife when she sees a wasp.

Chapter 6

The phone call
that said, "sit."

Not long after the coffee and the reflection came the phone call that everyone must dread.

It was now Friday the 13th, no joke, the day after the encounter with the shadow figure. The phone rang and I picked it up. On the other end of the line was the girlfriend of my best friend Mick. Her name was Sarah and I had only met her once.

Mick had been an ever present in my life since I was around fourteen- years-old. We had, in fact, known each other since we were eleven when I replaced him being the new kid at primary school, but our friendship didn't blossom straight away. In fact, it took three years until we occupied the same classroom at secondary school. We had drifted apart a little in recent years, but he had always been someone you could rely on. He was my ex-school buddy that I shared so much of my past with, so many good times and never a falling out.

I had so many memories of him, lots were quite comical but some only with hindsight, including the time in biology where we had to find our own blood groups. We had to make ourselves bleed with an instrument provided by the teacher which didn't inspire me at all; I have never liked the sight of blood.

After a few minutes everybody seemed to have done this apart from me, I felt useless. Instead of a short sharp stab that was needed I tried to gouge out the blood like a coward and was butchering myself with the appliance. Mick noticed my difficulty, took the instrument off of me without a word and then told me that he would prick me with it in five seconds and to get ready. I closed my eyes and accepted my fate. 'Bang,' he had already got me by the count of two. It worked, the blood flow was good and true.

On hearing the voice of his girlfriend on the phone, I was told immediately that I had to sit down. I felt like that schoolboy again but did as I was told. Then came words that I don't ever want to hear again in any circumstances. I was told that Mick had been killed the previous day just after 3PM. He had been riding his high- powered motorbike, it had been in a collision with a van and

Mick had died shortly after the impact. The collision was so fierce that he lost a limb in the accident. With a gasp, many of the images of Mick came flooding back to me like rapid fire as I felt my jaw drop at the same time.

I immediately knew what the shadow figure moment from the previous evening had represented, l didn't have to be Sherlock Holmes with an enigma of his own; I knew it was Mick coming back to me. He had the accident at around 3PM and had found me a few hours later at around 7.40PM.

Going back to around fourteen days before his accident, I was on my own at home when there was a knock at the front door. I opened the door and there was a man standing in front of me in full motorcycle gear, with his helmet still on. 'That's a bit rude,' I thought.

Then the penny dropped, it was Mick. It was just part of his sense of humour that I don't mind admitting had rubbed off on me more and more as we grew up together. I then did something that I had never done before in his company. I grabbed him and gave him a massive bear hug as if my life depended on it. As I did this, he chuckled to himself in recognition. The strange thing is that I am not usually a tactile person and rarely give other adults hugs of my own accord. They at least have to show willingness, otherwise I feel awkward.

We had drifted apart recently and yet here he was, back in my life once more. We swapped mobile phone numbers and agreed that we would go out as a foursome with our partners as soon as possible, which we did a few days later. It was to be our last night spent in each other's company.

On that day, some fourteen days or so before the accident, Mick had settled into our new leather settee and we started to talk alone. I still remember exactly where he sat and often look there in reflecting on how delicate our lives are. We started to catch up on all the things that had happened to us in the last couple of years.

It was at this time that I filled Mick in on the goings on in our house. He listened with an absolute open mind. He was an intelligent man and always was a leading brain in our top class that we once occupied together at school. He didn't give me a look that I had got many years before from the GP in front of my small son when I had repeated a true story.

Now I've got my faults like anyone but he knew that I was no wide boy that had to make things up to gain attention and have my ego stroked. This wasn't my character and I wasn't attracted to this type of character either.

At this point, I think I should enforce the bond that had been between us. This is something that I cannot over emphasize with the wisdom that has followed since these experiences. Living things have souls and, when the connection between the souls has been very strong in life, that bond will continue from them now in the spiritual realms. This does not matter here if we are talking humans or animals because animals have souls too, all you need is an open and trusting heart and I maintain something will happen to you sooner or later. I never doubt this. However, it has a lot to do with the individual mindset of the person involved. If someone has the mindset of nothing ever impresses them then they will simply never be impressed, it really is that simple.

I would say the stronger your belief the better the connection. The big mistake is when something does happen don't brush it under the carpet and forget it. Make a journal and record the goings on, chances are you will keep adding to the experiences. I now have a very long list.

The bond and trust between my friendship with Mick had ultimate strength. We had been the best man at each other's weddings, unfortunately, his hadn't lasted and that's why he now had a girlfriend. We were comfortable in our own skin and comfortable with each other. We had been keen motorcyclists in the earlier days and clocked up vast amounts of mileage together, but my inner voice had told me to stop.

Although I liked sport and he liked fishing it was our sense of humour together that was the strongest bond. Our love of the sitcom 'The Young Ones,' really cemented our connection. We sat for countless hours in our youth watching VHS tapes of it. There wasn't one single episode that escaped us. In fact, if someone had muted the volume we could have quite easily continued with the dialogue until the volume was restored; with what we thought was the flamboyance of the actors involved. Mick often told me that he could never forget my birthday because it was the day that the fishing season started. He ate anything that came out of the sea and often gutted his own fish with the ease of a fishmonger. I had witnessed him do this as a teenager and later wished that I hadn't. He seemed to have a great fascination for the workings of all living things.

The ultimate trust came when I started my first serious relationship with a girl, called Debbie, but had to go on a family trip to France for two weeks. They shared a lot of time together in that two weeks before I came back because we had been a social threesome for some time. He never tried to overstep that mark, he was an ultimate friend and valued our friendship so much more than that.

Now, I had something to ponder over and it was troubling me; I had seen him as a shadow figure. Now ultimately I had the belief that if you saw something dark that you could not explain then that was bad. This was lurking over me for a few days because he had never done anything to my knowledge that would call for darkness and the despair that I had conjured up through my lack of understanding at that time that went with it.

This belief did not hold fast because within a number of days of his passing I was waiting to pick my daughter up from secondary school when I glanced up to the sky and looked at the clouds. I have always been someone who likes nature and notices things others may simply discard. I often look upwards during the day or night and just observe the clouds or the midnight sky.

As I looked up, waiting, I could make out two words very clearly in the clouds. The first one was my name, Grant. The second was the word free. That's it 'Grant free.' I can assure you that if I was going to make this up I could have come up with something much more mesmerizing and interesting than these two words. The event was, for me, another one of those loose jaw moments.

The only thing here was that my name was written exactly how I would use it in my chequebook or to sign my name, with a special looped 'G' of my own design. My immediate family and my bank were the only ones who knew this. I had no explanation for it.

The word free represented that Mick was free from his physical overcoat that was once his physical body, this was an expression I was to hear so many times in the coming years. It was a reference to death being the equivalent of taking off or discarding an item of clothing, freeing the soul to move on to a higher vibration, a different plane of existence. Some also refer to our human body as a body of clay when they are separated from it, only later to find themselves again reconnected.

When Mick had appeared before me the body language of this shadow figure suggested to me a complete ease with his new form and surroundings. There was a total calmness about him. There was no sense of panic, no alarm, just plain acceptance. I got the distinct impression that he had returned to a place that he had once come from, a place that we have all occupied. We come from a source and we return to it.

Chapter 7

Wanted or not that new path arrives

Those that have very little to hide often don't seem to mind a barrage of questions being asked and hence the limited ducking and diving around the subject matter will become clearly evident.

G.G.J.Sanders

When someone that you cared deeply about is gone from your life it feels so final, you are powerless. There is this deep feeling that when you venture from your front door after an event of this magnitude you somehow expect the birds to have stopped singing, or your fellow human beings will be walking quietly past with their heads down, with no laughter to be heard anywhere. The reality is that nothing externally really changes from one day to another and you have to bite that invisible bullet and cope as best as you possibly can.

So what do you do when your life has changed to a point where you have more questions than you have answers? For me, that was simple because my tail feathers felt very ruffled from all these different experiences that surrounded me. I needed to start learning more and quickly. I felt like a plethora of information awaited me and I was willing to build up knowledge. If I wanted to construct a wedding cake then I already had the base in place. I now needed additional tiers to see how everything stacked up. I was willing to listen and learn.

As a starting point, there was a female medium coming to a local venue from out of town. On that night and only a few months after Mick's passing, I was accompanied by my wife. We took our places and listened to the medium going solo on the platform talking about the spirit world. We found out that she had already written books and was therefore no novice.

The first thing she did was pick one person from the audience that she wanted to speak to; that person was me. I shuffled in my seat with nerves but kept a smile on my face as she started to communicate with me. She mentioned that my spirit guides were starting to draw close to me and influence my journey, like holding my hand. That was it, the message was delivered and she moved on.

When the night got into full swing the audience were encouraged to ask a question and then the medium would use her psychic skills to tell that person in-depth things about them. I decided that I didn't want to go first, but after that first person had finished I couldn't get a look in because hands were being raised left, right and centre and I regretted my initial plan.

In fact, one of the audience made themselves look very silly. This has turned out not to be rare but a recurring issue in many mediumship events that were to come. There always seems to be one who just wants to be very difficult, to make the medium look foolish and it often backfires.

A lady in the audience was told that she had a strong link with Germany. The lady denied it point blank and said she didn't. The medium insisted that she was being told by her guide that there was a connection with Germany. After what seemed like many uncomfortable minutes with people starting to focus their gaze out of the window with awkwardness, the lady relented and mentioned that both her children were born in Germany, with a very stern face. Now, why didn't she just admit it in the first place?

Another thing I clearly remember hearing was a question from a lady in a seat behind me. She asked the medium as to why is it that some people are blessed with a relatively painless death, whilst others suffer for a long time until they pass over.

'Ouch she has got you with this one,' was my immediate thought. The reply came swiftly and without much deliberation. She stated that we are all here to learn and grow and the ones that take longer to pass on are usually the ones that have not learnt all the things that they had to accomplish in this lifetime and so have to live longer in the physical plane. 'That was a fair point,' I thought. She hadn't even tried to worm her way out of the question like I had witnessed various politicians doing in my time. The answer had also come without anyone seemingly being offended by it.

The thing that shocked me was that after hearing this gifted medium talk I didn't want the night to end anytime soon. I felt a connection with what she was saying after the untimely death of my best friend and wanted to hear more and more.

I would urge people that go to see mediums live, that haven't been before, to view everyone's body language and facial expressions, just have a good look around. Good mediums will often not accept no as an answer when they are sure they are right and get to the truth by being persistent.

I have seen mediums not only bring out tears of frustration but also tears associated with happiness on many occasions. If this is people acting, then watch out at the Oscars is all I can say. In my opinion, one of the hardest things to do is lose control of your emotions on demand with the clear, evident flowing of tears.

When it came to the end of the night, the medium started selling her books to anyone that was interested. I thought that I would buy one but had no idea which one. I started to talk to a lady in front of me and explained that I was lost and did she know which one I should buy. She told me that she had already read one of them and had come for a signed copy of another. Her recommendation then led to the purchase; good old word of mouth coming up trumps.

You could have your own personal message written in your newly purchased book that night to make things informal. I was up for that and went up to see her when it was my turn. She asked me who to make it out to and I responded with "Grant and Allison," without helping with spellings.

Allison joined me at the front. The medium then looked us both up and down, signed and then closed the book and handed it to me. I turned with a smile and opened up the book and couldn't believe my eyes. On Allison's birth certificate it had been decided that her Christian name be spelt like the surname with two L's, it was very rare, so rare in fact that I would have thought that less than five percent of all Allison's would have it spelt like this in the UK. The medium somehow knew and spelt it like the surname, I was dumbfounded by this.

At this point Mick's funeral was still quite raw in my mind. This had happened at the end of October. I had immediately offered my services to his grieving parents for doing a eulogy, it was the least I could do, they readily accepted.

When they agreed so quickly I thought to myself 'I hope that I am not the only one standing up at the front to do this at the funeral,' I soon realised that I was, but it all went according to plan and the tears held out until just after my final word. Then, I indeed lost control of my emotions.

'The paradigm shift'

The reading of the book that I purchased that autumn night didn't take long at all. I had read it within a few days. Then it became book after book after book. Now, I realise that there are people that can read books very quickly but

I had read fifteen in my first twelve months, not bad for a person that hadn't been interested in reading at all. I must admit they were not all relating to the human soul at first, but soon I would read nothing else and stopped counting when I got passed fifty in this category.

It all became very natural when I discovered, what was for me, sublime subject matter. I felt it was so wrong of me to ignore so many intelligent people's views; after all you don't learn much in life without actually listening to what other people have to say. There were some books I read that I physically could not put down and this was all new to me. They were so good that you wanted your stomach to stop rumbling so that you continue rather than going into the kitchen to make a sandwich and having a breather.

I liked this new change in myself. Good things can come out of bad situations and this was going to be a good thing on the new path opening up before me, I was adamant of that. My rule of thumb became that if Mick had the respect to single me out after his physical death, then I needed to reciprocate that respect and have the self-discipline to look into all of this and make my own mind up about what existed outside our five senses.

After all the conversations I have had with people since 12/10/06 I would say that the general public fits into three categories when talking about the possibility of life after death. There are the ones that will put their palms out in front of their faces, they just don't want to listen; usually men. There is the second category that will listen and admit there must be some truth in it but they can't make their minds up. Then, the third who will look at you as if you have helped them, sometimes with tears in their eyes and may admit that something has happened to them that has bamboozled them too.

You will find the vast majority of the dozens of books that I have read since my experience in my bibliography. In fact, the thing that I started to realise was that if you imagine a large wagon wheel with large spokes and put all these subjects along the circumference the parable of all the books would seemingly meet in the centre of that wagon wheel. It was almost as if every author was singing from the same hymn sheet.

You then start to watch related programmes on television and comment on what's happening without blinking. Like understanding what someone is saying in a different language when previously you would have sat and scratched your head.

I should explain here that OBE's 'out of body experiences' are quite different to NDE's 'near death experiences.' With an OBE I should refer you back to the first chapter; it was what happened to MR.B. He left his physical body and his consciousness was now with him standing at the door rather than the figure seemingly asleep on the bed, his spirit had left his body possibly triggered by his ill health.

NDE's will usually happen around the time of the heart stopping. The only reason that we know about them is because the person affected has returned to their physical body, sometimes willingly and sometimes with an absolute determination not to return to this life but to stay in those heavenly planes.

Some report refusing to come back and feel a slam as they are reunited with the physical because they have no choice in the matter. After all, if it's not your time, it's simply not your time. Effectively, you have unfinished business that still needs to be addressed. You're journey (or destiny) that it is said you have already agreed with the higher power, prior to your birth, is incomplete and has to be completed. We all have a destiny.

Chapter 8

The impending accident involving my children

It's important to remember that events will
never make perfect sense until we actually
accept that they are happening to us and then
start to ask many questions as to why.

G.G.J.Sanders

I remember a female chat show host being questioned about parenting issues in an interview. She mentioned that she was first and foremost a parent and being a friend to her child came second to that. I pondered this for a short duration and thought that this kind of sums me up too.

During our time as being parents to our children, we make informed choices for them. This can be regarding anything and sometimes we are not popular as a result of this because younger children generally don't see the dangers that we do.

In the summer of 2007 we had agreed that we would all go to the coast as a family, including myself, my wife, our two children then aged sixteen and ten, with my mother who always insisted on driving her own car. The children had continuously pestered me about letting them go in my mother's car and I had said no to them many times but relented merely due to being unpopular regarding this issue. I was seemingly the bad guy. Sometimes if our children pester enough a 'no' can then turn into a 'yes.'

Previously, I had the opinion that if something was going to happen to my family whilst I was at the wheel then I could blame myself. Now the rule had lapsed I felt uneasy but realised that parents eventually have to ease off a little.

On the day in question, I had awoken with everybody else and from the moment I got up something was very different. The spirit noises that were associated with our house were on form to the extent that the atmosphere was charged; this being very evident to someone sensitive to the spirit world. All the noises seemed to follow me wherever I went both upstairs and downstairs. I can only liken this experience, to someone who has never experienced it, to that of a fly out in the fields on a hot day that spots a person and buzzes around them until only it gets tired of you. I wasn't going to be left alone.

Eventually, I got to the point where I started talking quietly that if I was being warned about something, to make a noise in the next five seconds. When the noise duly arrived I couldn't believe it. After many episodes of this I felt like I was being neurotic so I turned my questions inward with no words physically spoken (only thought) hoping that would be an end to it.

These noises coming from electrical appliances, the walls and my general environment continued within the time frame, my thoughts were now being invaded too. I then started to shut it out and effectively pretend that I was imagining all of this; it must be sheer coincidence I thought. The day then went ahead as scheduled. The first half of the day was enjoyable but uneventful in terms of any incident; there were no related problems to report.

I have to state here that we all have our own idiosyncrasies, my young son was no different. From a very young age, after his car-seat had become obsolete, he had the habit of getting in the back of the car and placing himself behind the front passenger and not the driver every single time. We had no idea why he did this, but we let him continue without introducing a change that would make him unhappy, disrupting the routine.

On the way back from the coast that day we had decided to have a pit-stop at a pub halfway along the return journey. I was driving our car and pulled into the pub car park waiting for my mother to take a right turn behind me. She didn't do this straight away and seemed to hesitate. All of a sudden a speeding car came over a dip in the road and ploughed into her car. The point of impact was just behind the driver's seat, being very close to a 'T' shape collision.

There was total silence in the air after the impact and I felt like my heart was in my mouth after someone had punched me in the solar plexus; it was an utterly horrible moment. My wife was the first to rush around to the car to find everyone conscious and coherent. Fortunately, the point of impact was on the opposite side of the car that my son always chose. If in fact he had been on the impact side of the vehicle it could have been a different outcome because the impact would have been absorbed by his small frame at point-blank range.

We got everyone out of the car and the staff from the pub rushed out and insisted on getting everybody hot and cold drinks at no cost, which was very kind. The police were then called and Insurance details swapped. Before it got to court everything was settled.

So I had been warned and didn't pay attention to it. I was very disappointed with myself. The one thing that was reinforced to me that day was that the spirit world knows our immediate future, they know exactly what is going to happen to you on a given day and they will be with you through the whole experience. There is always someone watching over our events no matter who you are.

Also, don't doubt that your thoughts carry no weight. One of the things I have learnt is that when we pray it is like sending an e-mail to the divine, we just have to hope that our message gets answered.

So when a few months after the accident we were due to make the seventy-mile journey to see my father and I had a vivid (but horrible) dream the night before, I acted on impulse.

In the vivid dream, I was driving our car and my actions behind the wheel caused the death of my wife on the way to see my father. So when I woke up to see her lying next to me in bed, untouched and unmarked, it was one of the biggest reliefs of my life.

In fact, I was so incredibly shaken, not only did I cancel the whole trip but insisted on dipping into our savings and buying my wife a necklace of her own choosing as a token of my love for her. My father could hear the emotion in my voice when I called him that day. He was calm throughout and just accepted everything that I was saying, but it was his way in life. Later, with his illness that claimed his life, he accepted that too, there was no fuss and no fight.

I am a person who believes that there is always someone that is better than you at something whether it involves knowledge, sport, work, playing an instrument; anything really. In a similar fashion, this includes all the experiences that I have had. Some of the things I have already mentioned in this book may sound strange to some, but I know that others will say "I can top these experiences," I have no doubt of this whatsoever. The real shame is when they don't share it. I reiterate that I feel it is my job to make people more aware by laying my hand on the table for all to see. I realise that I am laying my soul bare in this book and some will frown over my comments but feel it is essential to set everything in the correct light.

Here I will use the example of the shadow figure in an earlier chapter. There are people that have seen full body apparitions with light emanating from every pore of their presence, that have stood at the foot of the experiencer's bed. These apparitions may start off with what can be described as a rotating diamond of light that has entered the room and the presence then emanates from that light. These spirits are often deceased relatives who have then communicated not through an actual voice as we know it but by thought alone. This can then be heard inside the living persons head like internal stereo sound. Imagine having an experience of this magnitude and simply keeping quiet about it. The shame is I feel that many seem to do just that.

After the accident, I came to the conclusion that whatever had warned me had not only genuine thought for me but for the welfare of the whole family. It was love being offered to us all. When I related this back to the many goings on in our house over the years, including the levitation of that towel, I knew for certain that this was no haunting. In all honesty, I felt it was my maternal grandmother offering evidence of the continuation of the human soul as she had done with her 'olfactory ADC.' She had effectively tried to do this even before Mick's fatal accident.

Chapter 9

Things are about to change!

Although I was good at sport and played for my school football and cricket teams in my younger years, I was never going to earn a living from striking a ball. I started to analyse this from a different perspective and actually became quite thankful.

These athletes that have sublime hand to eye coordination and physical stamina in abundance are often rewarded handsomely. In truth, there are some that I admire but as a group they are often treated in our society like they can do no wrong no matter what their personality. Some can do things that make us question their morality and are then seemingly forgiven because they are idolised. Why is this?

On the other hand, do we know the person who gives vast amounts of their own blood over time to help save human lives and expects nothing in return? Do we know the person that always carries their donor card or will leave their body to medical science? What about the person who has worked endlessly for charities and raised hundreds of thousands of pounds that simply never seems to stand out from a crowd?

Certain areas of the media seem to take great delight in showing us a reality television character falling out of a nightclub taxi or finding the latest TV personality or pop star that has an alcohol or drug abuse problem. Personally I'm more concerned about the young child that goes to school but comes home to look after their sick mother or father alone. Shouldn't things like this be the main concern? Why haven't we got more television programmes that highlight their individual plight with millionaires getting ready to put forward money to help? Also, what about the family that will soon be evicted because the parents have lost their jobs because of something branded 'a recession?'

Some of the large companies that have seen their large multimillion annual profits fall by a few percent (remember they are still making huge profits) now feel they must sack people so they can still be seen as cutting edge. They are often getting rid of the very people that contributed to putting the company exactly where it is. Try explaining this to the young children soon to be out in the cold and why does that newsreader announce these companies slight fall in profits, on a year for year basis, like someone has died?

At this time, I was working two part-time jobs. One where I had my paranormal experience and my second job was as a white-collar worker. Like many families both the parents were working hard to support the children. Weekends become very important but were reserved for all the grocery shopping until Monday comes back with a bang. The cycle then continues and you wonder where the enjoyment fits into this life.

One of the things that we looked forward to as a couple was going to a beautiful place called 'The Arthur Findlay College' in Stanstead. This could be described as a spiritual college and once you enter through those big doors and later walked around the extensive grounds you somehow feel like you are at home. Here, they had various courses offered and once a year opened up for a specialised open-day weekend that ran into a bank holiday. You had around three to four days offered to find the one day you wanted to attend.

We would look at the schedule offered online and pick out the day that would suit us most. I preferred live mediumship so would be drawn to this. If you attended the course for the day but were not picked out by the resident medium you could always have your own private sitting for an extra fee.

One thing that I have learnt from many visits to see mediums is when the medium is talking to another person, open yourself up by closing your eyes and relaxing; tune out a little. You are effectively opening up a channel to help the medium come to you, making that connection. Since I have been going to group events I have been picked out more than once by doing this and have been nudged by my wife when the realisation comes that the medium was waiting for me to answer a question she was asking me as I opened my eyes.

Mediums do work differently and there is no set rulebook. Some will pick out a row and say "I am somewhere in this area," others will pick someone out and tell them that they want to talk to them directly. In my opinion, the ones that are less experienced will give the whole room information and many people will put their hand up. Then it takes many minutes to get, for example, six hands down to one so that the message can be delivered.

It was here at the 'AFC' that we discovered a female medium that we were both very impressed with, although the general standard is extremely high. The popular mediums appeared harder to book because people would come into the college, having been before, and immediately put their names down before the day starts properly. After all, if you know someone who is very good at their job you make sure you see them again. During our early visits, we often got one of the last available appointments.

On one particular sitting, after my maternal grandmother had again turned up for me out of the ether, the medium explained to me that the jobs that I currently had would both be gone within the next two years. She was using her clairvoyant skills to look into my future. I did want a change but thought this highly unlikely because jobs were getting harder and harder to come by. I then got the distinct impression that redundancy was on the cards for me yet again, it would soon become at least a hat-trick of redundancies.

Not only did she convey this information but she also told us that our house that we lived in was a hive of spiritual activity and relatives from the spirit world were constant visitors, making themselves known. I was very pleased that she was confirming my prognosis after the accident involving my children. Not only did she know all of this but she also told me that I was thinking over a business idea and seemed clued up on it too.

Within that timescale of two years mentioned by the medium on that day things had rapidly changed. My cashier job became very stressful, other staff had long-term health issues, and in them not being fit for work I was effectively on my own.

I raised a grievance because I had to work for long periods unaided when historically it had been a two-person job and now I couldn't cope due to the sheer volume of custom. I also had time off because of a virus I could not shake off, which usually happens when I do too much, and then I go under. My grievance didn't get very far so I handed in my notice and was gone by the next week.

Just after this my brother, who lived over the other side of the country, invited us all down for a few days. He had moved away from the family and attended university, then decided he liked the area after finding a girlfriend and simply stayed put. An inexpensive holiday is always good when you are on a budget so we took the offer.

On one of the days I had just put a temporary parking permit inside my car window, outside his property, when a guy pulled up on the other side of the road in a minibus; I watched on. He had come to pick up an elderly gentleman from a property and the minibus driver was very pleased to see this old fellow and greeted him with a lovely warm smile and genuine compassion. The old gentleman returned the greetings if a little more understated than the driver's enthusiasm. He was helped on the minibus and they pulled away smoothly. I could tell in a heartbeat that this guy loved his job.

I had looked on at this scene thinking to myself that to go out on a daily basis helping other people and enjoying what you did really appealed to me. I could see myself as the fellow lowering the step and lending a helping hand with a smile. It seemed so much better than my day sat behind a desk having almost daily nose bleeds; which I was later told on a first aid course by the lecturer that this was caused by stress. All I can say is these nose bleeds were soon to stop for good.

I returned to my only job left which was white collar work. People were always telling me that they would feel stifled in an office and I tried my best to ignore what was for me getting more and more obvious. We were soon to say goodbye to an older member of the team who I knew I would miss a great deal. We had many philosophical conversations about life when time would allow it.

Suddenly it dawned on me that her husband was involved with a local charitable transport company that used minibuses, maybe a kind word could be put in for me. Then one day, at the eleventh hour of her working life, my colleague got up to go for lunch. I watched her walk away and then it was almost as though two hands were pushing me along, one on each side of my back. This was meant to happen. I got up and literally ran after her. I felt like a child running at the local swimming baths soon to be told to walk.

I stopped her outside and explained that I wanted to make a difference in people's lives and I felt I could not do that at the moment. I was currently dreading coming into work and could she help me make that change by talking to her husband. I was amazed by her kindness that followed. She told me to have a CV and accompanying letter ready by the next day explaining why I wanted the job and, in a nutshell, she would see if she could find a listening ear.

I agreed; I have always tried to be as good as my word in life. Soon I had an interview. The interview then led to a written assessment and an extra driving test, to see if I could handle the vehicle, and the job was mine.

I started on a route transporting local teenage students to college but soon after I was offered a route working with learning disability adults, a testing role that I found requires a lot of patience and personality if you are going to make it work. I took the bull by the horns.

I felt very much at home with the idea as I had known a learning disability group on and off since I was fourteen-years-old. I was back working with a group of individuals that just felt like my family. After all, I had always just seemed to bond with them. I soon took to the job like a duck to water and no longer felt like a square peg in a round hole.

Going from a Business Support Officer to a humble Minibus Driver must seem like a crazy step to make but I was no longer interested in titles. My father gave me his blessing just as he was starting to get sick with his terminal illness so that spurred me on even more.

We checked our finances and realised that the main hit would be not going on holidays for a few years but better times do come along. If I had a list of priorities then having a holiday was lower down on my list than something like being happy and contented. Luckily, my wife has always had a similar thought process to me.

Chapter 10

Don't I know you?
This is all familiar!

If someone's destiny is far removed from the way they are living this life, for instance, they offer no love, compassion, kindness or generosity; then the logical conclusion, as far as I see it, is that reincarnation into a different life will keep happening until that destiny gets fulfilled.

G.G.J.Sanders

If you have had the feeling that you have been somewhere before or someone you know just seems too familiar, would the idea of reincarnation be too much to consider? After all, I already knew that my best friend had come back after completing a physical life.

I had thought previously that life wasn't quite right. Children were dying of starvation in one part of the world whilst another person could have everything they desire and live to be ninety. That simply made little sense and somewhere in the depths of my soul I knew there was more to it than that. I wanted to look deeper rather than touch the surface.

If you are not familiar with the concept of reincarnation, it is realistically being born, living a lifespan no matter how long, dying and then a rebirth usually in different circumstances.

An example could be a strong burly man that relied purely on his physical stature in his work and social life with little regard for knowledge from books. There could be a return to a physical life as someone that no longer had that physical presence and, because of this fact, reading books and learning had a much greater significance for soul growth. Another example is being a wealthy individual in one experience and then being born into poverty in the next life. For example, Imagine the irony of a wealthy politician obsessed with austerity measures who then comes back to a life where they constantly feel the financial squeeze.

Having had that life changing experience in October 2006 has a tendency to reset your clock and you now think about things from a different perspective. My view now became, 'okay let's throw any preconceived ideas I had out of the window and start from scratch.'

Reincarnation is a subject that had to be explored in my new question everything approach. I was soon to pick up books such as 'Children's Past Lives' by Carol Bowman, 'Soul Survivor' by Andrea and Bruce Leininger and 'Across Time and Death' by Jenny Cockell. All three of these outstanding books relate to direct family experiences of reincarnation that has encouraged an individual (telling the story) to become an author. I must confess these are some of the most absorbing books that I have ever read. Even if you prefer to watch films, as I once did, the last book has been made into a movie called 'Yesterday's Children' starring Jane Seymour.

It is extremely hard for anyone with an open mind to read books of this calibre and walk away from them whilst not taking the views offered seriously. I challenge you to do this. For me, if you are going to talk about reincarnation in the Western world you can rule out the idea of financial gain from the author for starters, quite a humble starting point in my opinion. After all, if someone wanted sheer commercial success wouldn't they try something like writing a biography for a person that was famous instead?

Religion is something of little importance to me personally. Through looking back in history, and even events today, religion can be associated with war and hatred and I personally choose to distance myself from it. We also often hear, through the media, too many stories regarding religious figures abusing positions of trust around the vulnerable.

I remember having a conversation with someone that thought the bible should never be questioned. So when I tried to tell them that I had read many a book on reincarnation and 'believed,' there was reluctance by them to even discuss this matter any further. Realistically, this was the same answer as putting two fingers in your ears, sticking your tongue out and blowing a raspberry until the other person stops talking. From my viewpoint, I will not be told how to think by any religious document that has preceded me.

My reason for saying this is that documents can potentially be manipulated. I ask the question why is there an old testament and a new testament? God is viewed to have different personalities in each, so which is correct? Did he send down a memo so things could be changed?

Why is there such a vast difference in the potential age of the earth in the bible as opposed to methods involving carbon dating? I feel that a face value approach would result in a conditioning of my mind when what does attract me more is giving myself in service to others. If I have got this wrong and my fate is sealed, I will await my future even though I have acted with kindness in the vast majority of life situations.

With my new found passion for information, I have read books that indicate reincarnation was indeed part of the bible but was removed many centuries ago. More than one book has mentioned the same year of this event 553AD. I have found the books by 'Carol Bowman' and 'David Icke' to be the most informative regarding this (see bibliography.)

My life has taught me that when human beings get entangled with power, their personal gain can become an ingredient thrown into the mix. I remember our own MP's scandal in Great Britain around a decade into the new millennium when some were manipulating their own expenses so that they could gain financially when already they commanded large salaries. When you are in a position of power integrity should be the highest accolade that you are seeking. I have learnt not to just trust someone because they are wearing a particular cloth or suit. In my view respect is something that is earned; it should never be an automatic process.

I am very open to a higher power or spiritual force but I believe it answers to us all no matter what it is; there is no prejudice involved by it. You only have to listen to people's accounts of NDE's to appreciate that even if they didn't believe in a higher power, such as God, they still felt unconditional love and witnessed those classic beautiful landscapes with vivid colours around them that are simply not available to us in this plane of existence.

The sceptic will intervene and say that everything that happens is the result of a dying brain, but all of a sudden they lose ammunition when certain cases come forward. There have been cases where the person going through the NDE with no heart beat and effectively clinically dead will be resuscitated and then recite conversations from the medical team around them after having no pulse. They also reveal, after this shift in consciousness, what their relatives were saying in a different area of the hospital in a similar time space to add to the enigma.

Strong evidence from individual testimonies should never be swept under the carpet. Some cases also go past a length of time that they would be considered brain dead because of lack of oxygen to the brain but miraculously are fine afterwards. Medical professionals such as nurses that work with those whose health is in decline, as well as hospice workers, would be amongst my first port of call if I wanted some meaningful insight of these issues. Who could give greater insight that someone delivering palliative care? After all, would you want to hear a film review from someone who hasn't seen that film?

Other areas that have intrigued are cases involving hypnotherapists where they have regressed a patient and without warning the patient has then spoken in a different language, despite never taking the time to learn it. The answer that I establish from this is that it should not be ruled out that this person has lived before. Sometimes these patients can be regressed into something called 'Superconsciousness.' This can be classified as relating to the soul itself. Through hypnosis, it has been found that there is part of the brain that stores the memory of life between life. Here if you imagine a sandwich, the bread represents the lives that the person has lived whilst the filling represents their life in spirit.

Proof, Proof, Proof

We are living in times where individuals come up with the word 'proof' and if they don't get that put across to them rather quickly then it's time to make a 'U' turn.

I cannot prove to you what I had to eat for supper yesterday evening but I know that my stomach was not rumbling when I went to bed. If you go on a vacation to a remote part of the world and forget to pack your electrical gadgets, how can you prove to your friends and family that you saw some wonderful things? You know what you've seen so in these circumstances aren't you the best judge?

In a court of law where we have the prosecution and the defence, the jury are making a decision on the evidence put to them. Seldom have this jury seen CCTV footage of an offence being committed. So does this mean that we should let everyone go free because absolute proof can't be guaranteed?

I can't prove that the man who died a year before my birth was my grandfather without DNA testing but like any other person I don't discount my lineage because of this. We can't keep coming up with the word 'proof' but only accepting it on our own terms.

If you have ever looked at a person that has been part of your life and had an inner feeling that this has been done before, what conclusion would you draw from this? There are at least half a dozen people in my life that I am sure I have known before. An uncle, a cousin, a younger child, a grandparent, there is something of a familiarity that can't be explained. When I have looked at them there seems to be something tugging at my heart, something that has been a puzzle to me up until now.

We can all be part of an established soul group. It has been said by many authors that in the spirit world we agree in principle to living a life where we become known to each other again. So who would coordinate some of these meetings? Well, largely a mixture of your spirit guides and your higher self, which is coded with information.

Reincarnation is an area where you may get some slightly differing views even by firm believers. For example, some may explain many lives lived by one person as like a long set of steps going up a cliff face. You live a life and move up a number of steps based on the difficulty of the life you have just lived and that you have to live a certain amount of lives before you graduate spiritually. Others will say that you can live one life and don't have to return if that is what you wish.

From my viewpoint, I agree more with the first example. It seems very logical to me that If we have shown that we are incapable of love, respect, kindness and companionship then we have not grown and will have to come back to learn more lessons. Therefore, I see some that graduate spiritually more quickly than others. For me it explains how different and diverse human beings can be, you get to appreciate this every time you watch the news.

Every now and then, it seems, an advanced soul will be born and will be recognised by millions. Sometimes they are with us for many years and at other times their life may be relatively short. I recognise Princess Diana as an advanced soul; the world simply took her to their hearts because they saw nothing but goodness. Sometimes, we as humans can override the kindness switch that we have. Some may feel that if their life is not going according to a plan, then why make an effort?

Princess Diana demonstrated to me that kindness is always a strength and never a weakness. So therefore, when I think of Diana I see a remarkably strong woman. I recall seeing all the floral tributes at Sandringham, close to where I live, as I drove past in 1997 after her physical death. The vastness of the public emotion and sympathy will stay with me forever.

Chapter 11

Meeting some wonderful souls

As I mentioned in a previous chapter, I first came into regular contact with adults who have a learning disability when I was fourteen-years-old and have now turned full circle. When I was younger and perhaps more impressionable about a career, after a redundancy, I wanted to get involved with a job that I felt I could do using a talent that I felt I was given. I actually trained to be an accountant.

Despite passing a host of exams, it never materialised for me. I had the qualifications but no office experience to speak of and everywhere I tried they seemed to want accounts office experience. There seemed to be no employer that I tried that wanted to welcome me as an individual based on my own merits.

Sometimes we train for a future in a career that we think we want and all of a sudden things change. We may work the job for a while then it dawns on us we are in the wrong job. What we have to put up with isn't what we felt the romance of the career offered. Like my previous job that I got out of with help, it simply didn't feel right inside and after working there for a few months I picked up a feeling of gloom that was starting to affect my happiness. For me happiness is something that is a prerequisite, I can't function if it is not there. Although I try and live by the old cliché 'smile though your heart is aching,' sometimes people can see through your defence systems when you are not happy.

It was like being on that train in and out of a major city and looking around and seeing one or two souls with gloom written all over their faces. You get a sense of their job paying all their expenses and more but you could feel something being taken from them. On these trains I have noticed that smiles are at a premium. I didn't want to be a person that did things they had to until they retired but through stress found that retirement didn't actually come to them.

In my new job, I was soon introduced to a new group of people with learning disabilities. The moment I was first introduced to one person in particular they rushed over and I will never forget that greeting. Since that day, I have witnessed a show of gratitude that I have found wanting in many other positions of work.

In my now much-loved job, I have a morning round and an afternoon round. I am usually responsible for a group of adults, by myself, taking them to their day centres and back home again later in the day. It is a job that I feel completely at home with. I feel personal responsibility for them and their safety and actually feel like a father figure, even though some of them are, in fact, my elders.

I don't feel at ease until I have either escorted them to their centres or safely home. I even prefer to exit the vehicle and hold open doors so that I know my good friends are safe and in the warm. The things in life that I feel most comfortable with are being a father, driving, sharing a smile, being sociable and bringing out my caring nature. Hey presto, I could use all five things in one job.

Not too many years ago there was an international football manager that criticized people similar to my group when being interviewed. In essence, he was saying that because of the way they must have acted in a previous life they have had to come back and now pay the price in this lifetime; payback for their transgressions. Quite a bold statement for a public figure I thought at the time who should have probably been talking about the next match instead. Indeed, if I had been interviewing him at the time, I would have liked to ask him how he could put a mark against someone's character without knowing anything about them.

I find views like this not only insulting to vulnerable people but completely off the mark too. During my own search, I have found that the complete opposite is true. The premise that I have found through reading a substantial amount of books is souls like the ones I work with have potentially lived many lives before. As more advanced souls, they come back and live their lives to show us how to love beyond our immediate family and to love each other unconditionally.

Someone with a learning disability has a soul just as sublime as anyone else that inhabits this earth. Down's syndrome, for example, is a human condition and all we are doing as souls are having human experiences. Learning disability individuals, like all of us, are encouraged by their spiritual guides to pick

80

future families before conception, whilst still in the spirit realms and I feel they choose really well because the families they are born into often love them to pieces. I feel privileged to witness that love every day on the doorsteps of many homes.

As souls, we often choose a life that fits the lessons we have attributed to our soul growth. Unfortunately, not all lives can be an easy path for us or of a clear rosy future. Often, if we did not have troubles or upheavals we simply wouldn't learn from that experience.

One of the many reasons we are here is to learn things about ourselves and others through life situations. Everything we have done and every thought that we have had in this life can be replayed to us when we pass to spirit in something called 'the life review.' Is this hard to believe? Well, those that have had a NDE often talk at length about things that they had done and forgotten about when they have their reviews. Your life as you have lived it becomes part of something called the akashic records (more about this later.)

In a spiritual sense, learning disability individuals have been there done that and got the T-shirt. They choose a life that other souls with lesser understanding would not be ready for. We can learn so much from them if we are only willing to take that first step.

If you haven't interacted with a person of this group you will often find a wonderful nature and a deep sincerity. They do not appear to have a nasty bone in their entire body. If they feel that they have upset you, when in fact they haven't, there is always an attempt of such a kind and warm apology, when what I have found in other environments, is that sorry seems to be the hardest word.

They often have such electric and mesmerising personalities and they love to have a joke. So I try very hard not only to make them laugh but be their DJ too, playing them music they like on our many journeys together to encourage bonding as a group.

When the conversation turns to celebrities and who they like I will often chip in with one of my impressions, depending on who they are talking about, to make them laugh. I will bring out Michael Caine, Bruce Forsyth, Paul Daniels, Johnny Vegas, Dame Edna Everage, Albert Steptoe or Inspector Blakey and wait for the laughter.

You can gauge how much you are valued by seeing the smiles on faces when you return after being away for a week or two. You really can't put a price on that because it lifts your soul. If I can put a smile on a face I just see it as part of my job. After all, I am the first and last person that my group see outside their homes. They have every right to feel wanted and respected and that starts with me.

As a group, they have little desire for money. All they seemingly want out of life is to be loved, have a safe and warm home, to attend their centres and have breaks away and trips out. They are not perfect (as I confess about myself) but often radiate love and affection.

There is so much that we take for granted. A loving partner to go home and cuddle up to, a car to take for a drive if we feel stifled and a job that can possibly see us save for many material possessions and holidays all over the world. The learning disability group often have none of this but still seem to remain happy and loving. Sometimes I do not understand how they do it. Most probably it is because they are finely tuned to their soul's purpose.

In my journey, I have found that 'old souls' have little desire for sheer materialism. After all, I have heard many stories of poor communities from underdeveloped countries that are willing to share what little they have with anyone who is in need.

Chapter 12

It was cosmic?!

Cosmic ordering relates to positivity and making your desires come true by having a positive mental attitude. You are effectively placing an order for yourself with the cosmos (universe.) Some of this ideology relates to either writing something down or saying want you want out loud and that thing will come to you depending on your desire not being too outlandish.

Cosmic ordering has worked for me on numerous occasions. When I was nineteen-years-old I had already gone through a few brief relationships that only seemed to last for around three months and then would fizzle out. At that time, I actually felt like my soul was aching because I find it hard to function without companionship. I felt that what I wanted in terms of love may be around in a year or more, but I couldn't wait. I wanted my 'soul mate' and quickly. I can quite honestly say that if I was offered ten thousand pounds or my soul mate I would have chosen the latter.

For some reason and I don't know why, I had the desire to look out of my bedroom window and speak out loud, with an aching soul, about what I wanted. What I said was something very similar to the following: "I am fed up with all these three-month relationships and want the next girlfriend to be the one." Then within a number of weeks everything changed.

I soon met Allison (my wife) and we have been together ever since. If you had asked me what cosmic ordering was back then in early 1988 I would have looked at you blankly and shrugged my shoulders.

We met when I had a strong desire to venture into a pub where I knew none of the locals, with a friend beside me. Allison was in that very pub. Again this is evidence to suggest that we meet certain people at certain times in our lives that can be pre-ordained. I must add these meetings do not always have long-lasting positive outcomes it depends on what we have to learn from them.

If you want your life to change for the better where cosmic ordering is concerned you must have the ability of self-analysis this is of the utmost importance. Kick out the negative and bring in the positive, think of ways to change your outlook. Admit your own faults to yourself because we all have them.

Self-analysis, I believe is very hard for us to do. For instance, it is the job of the police to effectively make us accountable for our actions. Have you ever tried to make someone accountable? I have and you often get hostility in return. After a while, you learn to leave it to the professionals.

I can remember being pulled over by police for going faster than I should have in my twenties. I remained polite but was a little annoyed not only at myself but them too. I found it hard to take the financial hit because I was a young father and effectively still a trainee (long before the minimum wage.) With age on your side and looking at the bigger picture you learn to understand that you were wrong, you pay the fine not dwelling on it; self-analysis taking effect.

Looking back I also cosmic ordered our end terraced home at the start of the millennium too. I would lie on my bed at the flat we owned and imagine that the ceiling I was looking at was not the ceiling of the flat but the ceiling of our next house that I had not yet seen. I tried to convince myself that if I got up at any moment and say reached for the kettle then I would be standing in a different kitchen and looking out of the window with a fresh outlook. I was in a meditative state when I made my order which can often help. I would mutter under my breath about what I wanted and I got it.

The last thing that I ordered was my change in job. I would go and walk my dog and whilst walking would speak out loud about my unhappiness and how I needed a job to make me genuinely smile again. I was again rewarded within weeks.

In essence, I would advise you to be specific about what you ask for and I do prefer to ask rather than write things down. Maintain your focus, this can be done by meditation. When meditating I like to breathe in through my nose for five seconds, hold it for another five and then breathe out through my mouth for ten seconds to help me relax. Do that a number of times and feel your body truly relax and your heart rate go down.

With meditation, the everyday pressures must disappear for a time, as they will return after you finish the meditating so don't let them spoil it. Think of it like going into work and leaving your troubles on the doorstep. Those troubles aren't going to disappear, so don't think of them until you pass them again on the way out.

You always need to keep your ears and eyes open in life, it's one of the things I swear by; cosmic ordering is no different at all. You may need to be part of the cosmic ordering equation yourself. Things will often not work out for you if you are not willing to put in the effort yourself, you can't simply sit at home with your feet up and expect miracles to happen.

In my change in job, it involved a little cause and effect. I had to talk to a work colleague to get the ball rolling and the reward was the potential job soon became mine. If you feel a natural urge that something is right then very often it is. Another key is to always have faith, you may not always see all that is working in your favour, but as long as you don't get greedy you should see some positive results.

Now, I have the utmost respect for authors that talk about cosmic ordering and positivity. However, there remained one thing that was important for me to understand regarding cosmic ordering in my new question everything approach. I had been asking for all these things and I received almost all of them back, but what if I want to say a big thank you, who did I say it to? I am saying that something or somebody has listened to me (often with that aching soul) and acted. It has acted on my behalf with love and compassion.

Now I believe the answer has revealed itself to me. I shall address this in the next chapter.

Chapter 13

She saw an angel

When we feel like we know all there is to know and no one, no matter what their station, can teach us anything new or provoke our thoughts in any way, then what we are dealing with is little more than human ego.

G.G.J.Sanders

My stepmother was very much a matter of fact woman, I remember my dad telling me that she had given him an ultimatum of ditch your two kids before I will take you as my husband. He refused, but then still married her when I was about nine-years-old. He only told me of this reluctance to accept me and my sister when I was an adult, although the signs were always there. Generally speaking, it was of little relevance because we always lived many miles away from their home that they shared. She didn't have much opportunity to show her true colours on a daily basis.

I'm not into character assassination of an individual, although I do believe in truth. After all, people do make mistakes and I'm no different from anyone else. My rule of thumb has always been I will try and meet anyone well beyond the middle of a line (that is between two people) but if someone does not make that effort to come anywhere near the centre what can you do? As in this case, they have effectively made their mind up that they don't like you without making effort. When you are a child and put in this particular situation you feel the pain of rejection in your soul.

I remember my father telling me that her first husband had collapsed and died in his forties. He had found out about an affair and drove his car around to the property of her lover to address the situation. As soon as he stepped out of the car to sort things out, he collapsed and died of a massive heart attack.

So why had my father settled for this? Well, we are all individuals and we can all make decisions both good and bad. Despite being a tall, dark and handsome man he did not appear to have female attention addressed his way. This was such a shame because he was a perfect gentleman and had respect for anybody and anything that crossed his path.

Their relationship had started when an uncle of mine failed to turn up for a date with her and my father had simply been around and mentioned that he would step in and take her out. It seemed the kind-hearted thing to do.

Much later, when I went to see him with my wife and children, my stepmother would either stay in her bedroom the whole time without saying hello or go out before we arrived. I remember seeing family photos around but none were ever of us and our birthdays were never written on their visible calendar. I presumed that none of this was permitted as she obviously ruled the roost. Her favourite quote was, "There is nothing as queer as folk," I found this phrase quite ironic coming from her lips.

During the last few years of her life, there became lots of pain and discomfort. She rarely ventured from bed or her armchair during these times. One thing that I have to mention is that she was always coherent. She never gave the impression of being under any type of strong medication. My father would attend to her every need but, when we did see her, she would often lose her temper with him when things didn't meet her exact criteria.

I do remember ushering my father to one side and asking him if he felt that she would deliver that love and affection if the circumstances were reversed. He answered with "No she would be off." He continued that love and respect right until the very end.

When it came to the Christmas before she passed over, I was again thinking of presents for them both. I would always get my father something to do with history or the olden days. I remember getting him books about old cars and what places used to look like before the war. I found that he was very easy to buy for.

With my stepmother, on the other hand, I had literally run out of ideas. I came across a book about contacting your guardian angel and something told me to roll with it. At this time of my life, I had no reason to believe in angels. I had not read any books regarding this subject and to me it was a bit of a grey area.

Over that Christmas period and approaching the New Year the phone rang, my father was on the line. He sounded very pleased to speak to me, you could always feel a warm glow in his voice. Then, he stopped in his tracks and told me that my stepmother wanted a word. This had never happened to me before and I immediately thought 'oh my, what have I done?' I was not expecting her to discuss the pleasantries of the day and I was about to be proved correct.

My stepmother then started to talk to me and almost demanded an expla-nation as to why I had got her a book about communicating with a guardian angel. I started with "Well;" when I need a second or two to engage this gives me that valuable time space. I then told her that I believed deep down that the book could do her some good in her current plight.

Her response was that she wanted to know who had told me. I told her that I had no idea of what she was talking about and started to feel that the conversation was getting a little tense. When she was reassured that I had no knowledge of what she was talking about she relaxed a little and told me something that I had not expected. She said that her illness had got to such a stage that she was finding it very hard to cope, so much so, that her pain had been at a level that she blurted out "God please help me;" just those four words. This again was the asking of something with an aching soul that I addressed in the previous chapter. Then, she told me that literally within seconds an angel appeared in front of her. I could feel the wonder in her voice but she was reluctant to tell me anything more.

I have found out that angels can appear to us in many different guises, you won't always see a being surrounded by light with a vast wingspan and I will never know exactly what she saw that day. However, she would not give the phone back to my father unless I told her whether I believed her or not. I told her that I had no reason to doubt her and so my answer was "Yes," I did believe her. My stepmother then handed back the phone to my father and the subject was never approached again, although I admit I would have talked about it in a heartbeat if she had ever pressed.

As I said before, my step mother was a straight talking woman. Some people in life are prone to exaggerate and although she had faults this was not one of them. In this respect, she was like my maternal grandmother. If she had something to say she would say it regardless of who was going to be offended, it was all part of the personality. However, my grandmother was like a cough sweet there was sometimes a hard exterior, after all she had six sons to be mother and father to, but she had a very mushy centre. Children were always a weakness of hers. The amount of times she looked at me as a boy when I had said something innocent and then said, "I could eat yer" with a heart melting look on her face were too numerable to mention.

As previously stated, it was my intention from the outset of this book not to have a religious theme because it is my firm belief that we do not have to believe in a higher power for it to love us and be ever-present. There is unconditional love for us, but we must try and be the best we can be not only for our own soul growth but for each other too. If we at least try treating each other like cherished members of our own family, life would be so much better for all concerned. After all, there are many that believe 'we are all God's children.' For me, this means that we are all family. If I were to look at the wider implications of this statement it suggests to me that our children are God's first and ours second.

I have had countless people say to me over the years that when they go abroad the locals are lovely and they don't get the same feeling at home. I feel if we all did at least five things every day in the thought for others, my thinking is that this comment would be a thing of the past. It can be as little as holding a door open for a mother and child, passing on good quality clothes to charity or helping an old person struggling to find a trolley at a supermarket. I have found that many seem to appreciate politeness, even if they don't say thank you afterwards, but we don't all want to give politeness back. You can witness this every day if you have ever worked front of house as I have. Sometimes rude and abrupt customers can wipe the biggest smile off of a person's face.

Personally, I have started to feel more comfortable using the word 'God' even if that sounds topsy-turvy. I have my own view and relationship with the divine despite religious documents telling me what it should be. My stepmother has helped make this transition with this terminology even though I would have never known her story if I did not buy her that book. Strong evidence again that suggests things happen in our lives for a reason. If angels had forgiven her for her behaviour towards other people's children, then the divine must have forgiven her too.

If I had not purchased that book for her maybe this book would not have been written. Certainly, I would not have read the mesmerizing book 'Angels in my hair' by Lorna Byrne without my stepmother's story and, if you want to start your angel journey somewhere, I highly recommend it. It's certainly a great start on getting a new perspective on things that the vast majority of us don't always see with our eyes.

If you feel uncomfortable with religion as I do, my message to you is do things your way. You are loved by an unseen force even if you don't want to acknowledge it as being there. The divine has unconditional love for you. My rule of thumb is if I want to address the divine I don't need to get on my knees to do it and I don't need to visit a church. It is my belief that those that are interested in cosmic ordering are already doing this just through positivity.

I have a similar mindset with visiting graves. The soul of the person you are visiting is no longer attached to those physical remains, they just represented the vehicle of life. Personally, I much prefer to get out old photographs of my loved one at home and talk out loud or say a short prayer in private. My understanding is they will hear your words just the same. At the end of the day it is all about personal choice, I don't feel comfortable grieving in a public place.

That experience with my stepmother has made me pick up other angel books. I'm here to tell you that your guardian angel (or main spirit guide as the terminology others may prefer) is constantly with you. There are guides that come into your life at certain stages, which can be your deceased relatives, who always want the best for you. However, your guardian angel has always been there and will be with you beyond this life. Who do you think will be next to you when you have your life review? You guessed it.

I soon started to understand that if you address your guardian angel and use the connecting word with the higher power, which my stepmother had done, you are instructing your guardian angel to act on your behalf. I referred to it in a previous chapter as the equivalent of an email to the divine, this message gets received. The word used was 'God' but I strongly feel that if anyone believes in an alternative religion the reaction would be just the same.

The penny has dropped for me about the connection between cosmic ordering and angels. People that use cosmic ordering are indeed being listened to. However, who is doing the listening? It is your guardian angel, your main spirit guide.

Cosmic ordering is all about positivity and not religion. Yet these people are still being connected to the higher power. I should know because I was one of them. It is common though that you will only get to see an angel under the most extreme of circumstances. Indeed many will only be seen as part of a NDE.

Chapter 14

The flickering screen

If something comes out and crosses your path
slow down and observe things because it is
likely that something else will be coming
across in quick succession.

G.G.J.Sanders

There are many mediums who state that everyone is psychic to a point, which I feel is accurate. Since having many experiences and now being very open and receptive, I started to have dreams that began to come true. These were seemingly just random things that I had little control over.

For instance, in one vivid dream that I had I was driving this Mini car and when I came to a junction, with my window down, there were five Mini's in a row trying to pull out one after the other. I knew that I didn't own this car so I just assumed I had been given permission to drive it. This chap came past the open car window and pointed at me and told the person who he was walking with that I didn't own the car, but everyone else in the line did.

As I felt he had got this correct I pulled the car over once I got around the corner, ran up to him and asked if he could tell me anything else. He was friendly and immediately got up close to my face and said in a clear voice "Yeah the football is going to be 0-0." With that, I was instantly awake with a jolt.

Now, the England football team were playing in the next 48 hours and I was planning to watch it. I went into the bookmakers and had a chat with the two guys behind the till and a few minutes later I was clutching a slip and kind of wondering why. To my surprise the result was the same as in the dream, I still have a photocopy of the winning ticket and now others to add. I only choose to bet when given information as I am not really a gambler, and it's sensible to have a limit.

During 2009, I started to have other different experiences that I had never had before. All this happened during a time which is referred to as 'The twilight state.' This is basically when you are almost drifting off to sleep or just about to wake up and open your eyes, for me it was always the latter. I must state here that although I have just talked about dreaming, this 'twilight state' is nothing to do with dreaming you just know that you are awake.

Before I explain in more detail, all human beings have seven major Chakras.

Chakras, put simply, are energy centres located in and around the body. Chakras act as conduits between you and the higher power.

I will list up to two things associated with them, but there are more. First is the crown chakra (around the top of your head) which is your connection to the divine. It is rumoured that your soul leaves your body through your crown chakra at the point of physical death. The third eye is next, which is the chakra that I want to focus on shortly. It is located roughly between your eyebrows and is to do with psychic and clairvoyant ability.

The next is the throat chakra which is related to speech and expression. Then the heart chakra, which is to do with love and compassion. Next comes the solar plexus chakra, level with your diaphragm, to do with control and personal power. The penultimate chakra is the sacral chakra in the lower abdomen to do with sexual energy and emotions. The final one of this list being the root chakra and is situated in the genital area when seated in the lotus position. The root chakra represents survival and security.

In total, I had four experiences within a limited timescale that involved my third eye when I was in this 'twilight state.' The first happened in early 2009. I was just about to open my eyes when I saw an internal screen located in that spongy part of your head just slightly above your eyebrows in the lower part of the forehead.

I jumped but kept my eyes closed. I had never seen anything without opening my eyes before. I saw an illuminated bright screen. I say bright, but the colour seemed to be pale, just bright by the illumination glowing around it. It was like looking at unmarked, plain wallpaper that was framed by something like a glowing picture frame.

I got the feeling that an image was just about to appear on this screen and as soon as this happened, I blocked it out because whilst I was having this experience it felt as though I had company. In essence, I was afraid that somebody was in the room with me and ready to hit me with something. Of course, it turned out that I was just unnerved, but by then, the screen had gone and wouldn't return, which left me very frustrated. I now wanted to know what would have happened next, like a child with a new toy.

The second time it happened I was ready. It happened on the morning of 17th May 2009. I saw what I can only explain as a cartoon type reel on the screen. If you are old enough to know this it was like watching the introduction of the show 'Grange Hill' around the year 1978, just before the acting started. That is the only way I can explain it.

Images in black and white were moving fast (vertically) from top to bottom. I actually saw an image of myself in one of these frames only much younger but the images were moving at such a speed that I could not keep up. It was like looking at 'The Generation Game' conveyor belt at warp-speed and trying to keep up with the progress and naming the things that passed by. It was impossible. A click on the wall in our reality came near my head just approaching the end for no apparent reason. However, from previous experience in my house I personally relate these noises to visitation from the spirit world.

The third time it happened was on 11th October 2009. This time the cartoon type reel was in colour and moving from left to right, much more like that 'Grange Hill' intro already mentioned. This time I was seeing images of things that I viewed in life actually on television but this television replay, as it were, was part of my third eye.

The last time it happened was just before 2010. It happened on 29th December 2009. The images on the colour screen were not moving as such anymore but flickering very fast. I saw a lot of children, then all of a sudden it stopped and I saw an image of this old tree which looked lonely and bare. This plain and almost ugly image of the tree was then replaced.

Second after second this most beautiful pink blossom, the most beautiful blossom I had ever witnessed, started to fill this empty tree, pop, pop, pop in random places. All this happened very quickly until it was brimming with amazing colour, a really vivid pink.

The only message that I can relate from this experience was that at this time I had just finished teaching a small group of children GCSE maths privately. I eventually found out that they had all got at least a 'C 'grade. For me, the message was spiritual. I was being told they had all passed; I had helped these children blossom.

The children all had two things in common. They were all struggling with the subject before but they were also fighters with grit and determination, attributes that had my utmost respect. They had all seen maths as something they needed for their future because it is one of the more highly valued subjects. It was not an option for them to fail it. One of the students was unsure how to add 2Y to itself at the start of mentoring and went on to get a 'C' grade. Another was expecting to get an 'E' grade and actually obtained an 'A.'

The thing that intrigued me was when my daughter Abigail went on to experience what I call 'the flickering screen' in her early 20's although we had never even discussed it. It made her feel very uneasy (as with me) that very first time. I reassured her that she was having these experiences because she was 'open' and her guides thought it was time for her to experience something spiritual.

I am confident in saying that this 'flickering screen' is like a 'mini life review,' but there is no reason to fear these experiences we have both had. In fact, the more it happened the more I relaxed and wanted it to return. However, it would be years before I had the experience again.

'The Design'

There are many songwriters who get their inspiration from a dream. In these circumstances, they claim the bragging rights but did they write the song? I have even had this happen to me. I have heard a wonderful song in a dream that I have never heard before, but when I wake up it is always slightly out of reach. I'm no songwriter so feel the experience was wasted on me.

It appears that the seed of the song has been planted and all the songwriter has to do in this particular situation is watch that seed grow in front of them and benefit from the ripe end result. I find issues like this to be spiritual because the work has seemingly been done. For me, it's like going into work and working on a report but before you go past the threshold to your desk, the report is then put in your hand yet the work is somehow yours. This doesn't happen in our own reality, so why don't we collectively question it when answers come in a dream?

My mind actively wonders when I think about similar issues. I often wonder how I could communicate the information I have gained to a young thinker. Maybe getting that keen brain thinking earlier and thereby planting the seed in that grey matter. After all, there is no reason not to question. How many times do teachers or doctors explain something about the human body and then state, "It's because of the way we are designed." Is this done as a generic statement or do they acknowledge a more spiritual understanding?

When I think about the higher power, that force in charge, that some refer to as 'God' I like to think about it like this: when a house is built or a car is manufactured there is always a blueprint. There is a person who has been working behind the scenes, often not known to us as the consumer, who has decided what goes where and how things sit. Whatever their job title they are effectively the designer; everything they achieve has started with a blank page.

The car has shock absorbers like our human cartilage ready to protect from forces that can damage. Our heart is like the car fuel pump and our blood is like the fuel for the car. To nick a vein is like a pipe leaking; the liquid can escape that helps propel it. Putting the car in gear is like our human brain being put into gear and the force will soon be available to create the motion to drive forward. Expect niggles and complaints relating to an ageing vehicle but also your vehicle of life (your physical body.)

The car has its own unique reference which is etched into the bodywork and so do we it's called DNA. Like the car, we also have an internal stereo but it is up to us if we take the time to tune it and hear what will come out of the speakers. The divine is the source, the creator that has thought about the plan and then implemented it.

Who else could have put our human design in place? I can assure you that somebody did. Should we seriously believe that this is all coincidence? We have two hands to help experience touch, two different ways of drawing oxygen into our bodies, two ears to hear with, two eyes to see with and taste buds galore in our mouth. If we lose one option then we always have a backup because of our design.

It's so easy just to accept, and many do, that we are here once, don't question anything just live life hard and fast. Make lots of noise and scoff at the ones that actually stop and think. After all, one of the main lessons that I learnt from five years at secondary school was in just observing my fellow students. Could it possibly be that the ones who make the most noise aren't necessarily the ones we should be listening to? My son is living proof of this, a quiet unassuming individual who got 9 A* grades and 3 A's in his 12 GCSE'S and was later offered and accepted his place at Oxford University after completing his four 'A' levels.

Those that do horrible things can't hide it

Lastly in this chapter I would like to address those that seemingly have two sides to them. One being their persona that they like to portray in public and the real them that will manipulate anything they can for their sordid activities. I refer to it as an 'iceberg personality,' they only show you what they want you to see and the rest is hidden from view. As a man myself I find it deeply distressing when another man has acted in deplorable ways with children.

There are those who believe that all they have to do is commit these dreadful acts and then pray and ask for forgiveness, having the slate seemingly wiped clean for them to start again from scratch. They then feel forgiven to do things over and over, given carte-blanche to act as they want. Their rule of thumb seems to be commit abuse, pray to the divine, commit abuse and pray again.

My search for answers has told me that there is the law of Karma, which if it does not catch up with you in this life it will be waiting for you once the realisation dawns that life is indeed eternal. There are many different ways of explaining Karma, but I simply see it as 'what goes around comes around.'

With this law, no one can escape the things that have been done as they form the akashic records and, with the power of thought which becomes our voice in the spirit realms, nothing is hidden. You think of something and others are aware of your thoughts. While we exist in this physical form everyone is capable of change.

Chapter 15

We are of spirit

One of the statements that I have heard many times since my life changing experience is that we are all spiritual beings having an earthly experience. Our true state is referred to as being discarnate which is unattached to the physical body.

Every human being on this planet has an ethereal body. The ethereal body represents the real us. This ethereal body is flawless. If you have had any problems with your physical body in life such as being deaf or blind, have lost a limb, whatever the problem is, it is said that it will still not affect your ethereal body. For example, blind people that have had a NDE can report to being able to see for the first time until they return to their physical body, more evidence that the ethereal body is sublime.

When our ethereal body moves to the astral plane at the point of physical death everything is restored. In fact it is said that your consciousness will expand beyond the sum total of all the lives that you have ever lived, instantly you are more knowing.

With regard to our human brain, we don't use the fullness of what we are capable of. We haven't unlocked the secrets into how to utilize more, but it would be foolish to suggest we simply can't. The mind is what accompanies us from the earth plane, the physical brain being left behind.

Let me explain more about the astral plane. If you have ever had a dream that you have been sitting in a tree or on top of a roof and have just known that you didn't need to worry about falling, then you have visited the astral plane. I have had many of these, my body will glide through the environment and there will be an inner knowing that I have done this before, it feels so natural.

If you have ever woken up and can't move your physical body straight away with what is known as 'sleep paralysis' there is every likelihood that you have visited the astral plane and your ethereal body has not aligned with your physical body. This alignment is usually met by lying still and simply waiting for the adjustment. Some who experience this relate to having seen spirits.

Our physical bodies are connected to the ethereal body by something that is called the silver cord. The silver cord is extremely elastic and is deemed to stretch to infinity. When someone has a NDE this silver cord can sometimes be seen. It is said to originate from around the solar plexus area, but some say that it could be slightly lower than this and attached to the belly button, which to me makes sense.

With this view, we are born into the physical plane with the umbilical cord connected and when this is cut the silver cord is still attached. This silver cord that cannot be seen by our eyes in normal conditions is severed around the point of death to release us from our physical body. With this theory, the umbilical cord is severed at birth and the silver cord is severed at physical death. You are then back to the source, where you came from.

We leave a shell, the physical body, which effectively is now that discarded old overcoat that is of no use anymore. We feel nothing that happens to this old overcoat once our silver cord is severed and now cannot return to it no matter how hard we try. Spiritually it will make no difference if you are cremated or buried. Your soul moves to a different plane of existence.

If you recall in an earlier chapter I mentioned having a vivid dream concerning my grandmother. She told me that she no longer needed to eat or drink to obtain her energy; this is very poignant. Some souls that have moved into their new environment can't adapt to all this change straight away. There are ways on the other side of slowly introducing a person to their new way of life which entails a process similar to our eating and drinking for a duration. Everything will now become conducted by the power of thought, speaking through our mouth as we know it is no longer required.

The place that our soul inhabits can have a direct relationship with how we have conducted ourselves in the life just lived, but it is good to remember that the higher power is very forgiving. It is usually up to us to judge the life we have lived through the life review process, whilst our guides watch on offering unconditional love and support.

Our souls vibrate at different frequencies and there are many planes of existence. It is often said that there are seven planes to be inhabited after we pass to the world of spirit, but there could be more than this. I liken the change in state from our physical plane to the astral plane as like hitting a switch or turning a dial, it is regarded as instantaneous. I feel the best way to describe it is like tuning a radio. We are now merely on a different frequency, so all the people we have left behind are still tuned into the last station before the dial was turned. Therefore, it is very hard for us to interact with them.

The higher you get into the spirit realms that frequency will be adjusted again. Therefore it is possible for all these planes of existence to occupy the same space, there is no overcrowding like in our physical world. The highest realms are said to be occupied by Jesus Christ, Krishna, Zeus etc.

People often look up to the sky to talk to their deceased relatives, but they can occupy the same space as us. We just don't see them (see my poem in the next chapter.) They certainly do make themselves known in our house.

I once heard a medium communicate with someone in the audience who had lost their wife. They related to this man that his wife had not left him and was being reprimanded because she now had other responsibilities in the spirit world that were being neglected. His wife merely wanted to be with the person that mattered most to her and quite simply still did.

We all have responsibilities that we have previously agreed in our blueprint of life and when we pass over we have responsibilities that continue. This doesn't mean we can't return and try and interact with loved ones because we can, which helps explain all the activity I have witnessed.

One of the planes of existence is said to be in complete darkness and is a thoroughly miserable place to inhabit. The souls that are said to inhabit this realm are the ones who conducted themselves in such a way that light was not a part of them. The easiest way I can explain this is if you live your life full of hatred instead of love you will not have lived up to the promises you made before you incarnated; by overriding the values that you agreed to participate. Therefore, 'the Summerland,' as spiritualists describe it, would be too bright for these individuals because their life has not been encompassed with light. If we are segregated in our current plane of existence from someone who, for example, wants to inflict substantial loss of life then it seems perfectly natural that some form of segregation continues.

We must always remember that the higher power will not leave souls in darkness for eternity, you are never forgotten. We are all seen as children of the divine. Picture a father that has two children, one is always good and one is never good. The father still loves both children and in reality this is how we are deemed in spirit.

There are many characters here on our planet that make us continually question human nature. Think about how long ago someone treated you like dirt beneath their feet whether you had direct contact with them or not. All I can say is that from my experience of looking into this it matters greatly that we buck this trend. Those that have had a NDE can describe feeling the pain that they have inflicted on others through words and actions back on themselves and feel the torment they have caused.

We are all meant to learn lessons that our blueprint has in store for us and if these lessons get learnt, in my opinion, we will need to be born into a physical body less and less. The ones not willing to learn their lessons, that in essence they had already agreed to learn, will effectively need more teaching and have to stay behind until the subject being studied is achieved. This entails more journeys back to a physical life. If the school gates are being closed for some, they remain open for others that still need to be taught important lessons.

I try very hard to conduct my life according to all the L's love, laughter and lessons (learnt.) If sometimes I feel that I am falling short I remind myself to try harder. This, of course, doesn't mean that I always try hard with a person that won't let me in, I don't. If they, through their own eyes, see nothing but bad in me when I'm actually trying to help them, I will start with a new path and simply go down it and leave them to find their answers.

I have been in one or two situations where a sceptic has got angry with me for my beliefs. I soon remind them that it's not my job to convince them, it's their journey. The evidence that I present to you through this book truly means something to me and I have got here by going at my own pace since an event that turned my world upside down.

I personally believe that if you have a NDE with an altered state reality that is deemed unpleasant, in other words being sent to darkness instead of light, then you need to pull your socks up and change as a person. It is often a wake-up call, but we have free will if we want to ignore it and carry on regardless.

Some believers in God feel he shouldn't let all the things happen that do happen in this world. From my viewpoint, it is important to remember firstly that we live in a temporary state that is 'the physical.' Secondly, we as human beings have created our own environment together. I don't feel that God would be to blame for humankind not living in harmony with the planet, animals or each other.

Our own laws govern the physical plane and divine law governs the spirit realms. Collectively we appear to be leaving 'our mess' for the next generation but with reincarnation in mind we are actually leaving it for ourselves again to come back to and pick up all the pieces.

Chapter 16

Love: the greatest gift to give & receive

You can reach me

It makes me think, it makes me wonder why;
all you do, since I've been gone, is cry.
When you look out through the window and you stare,
can't you feel me, you don't stand alone, I'm there.
I am the glint of light in the room I arrive on a beam.
I will teach you, I promise to reach you, but in dream.
We have a reason, we have a purpose and that is love;
I've finished my role on earth I've been released like a dove.
Don't break down anymore, don't lay your soul bare.
Know this, I've moved on, you can reach me in a prayer.

G.G.J.Sanders

Arguably the easiest way for communication from the world of spirit to anyone is the vivid dream. It was one of the first jaw-dropping things that happened to me that helped to start my questioning and anyone who has ever had a vivid dream will tell you that they are so real to the person that experiences them. As I relayed in an earlier chapter, you can have vivid dreams and see into the future.

The important message to remember from the poem is to give love and try our very best to let go with love when someone passes away. How can I say that? Well, I can tell you that if I had not let my father go with love or my best friend go with love I could not continue my journey and do all the things that my life has mapped out for me. Is that selfish? I don't think so, after all, I can also say that if I didn't have this mental strength I would probably be a complete mess all day and every day.

What good would this way of thinking be to the people I love all around me? I could not continue to give my best as a husband or father. I could not be the person that is looked up to by my learning disability group and who is going to love my dog the way I do? Take him for his daily walk and pick him up and hug him; telling him that I love him with a Jim Carrey type expression. He understands everything, even the smallest part of human body language.

I am confident in saying that the special person you loved with all your heart and soul is still around you. If you have not picked up anything within the first twelve to eighteen months of their passing you may need to focus in a different way. You have already paid witness to my account of my best friend and how he proved to me the survival of the soul. In other ways, things can be a little more understated but still noticeable.

Let's look again at my father. The only thing that I really wanted from my father's possessions was his mobile phone. For me, it was something tangible, something he had spoken to me on so many times whilst holding it in his hand.

So much is the case that I often would ask him why he didn't use his landline. Something inside me told me that I had to keep it and cherish it.

Since I have had his mobile phone it has turned itself on, a number of times, from being off with no power going through its circuits and nobody even standing close to it. I can tell you that it usually takes a good poke with the index finger to achieve the sequence of events that cause it to turn on and a lovely little melody makes its appearance to warm my heart.

We have had many mobile phones through the process of time, but my dad's is the only phone that has done this. It is his link with me back in the physical plane that I am still part of. The phenomenon also comes with its own terminology 'a telephone ADC.' Some people even get to talk to the person that is regarded as deceased. So when I have this experience with my father's mobile phone I talk openly as if he had just entered the room.

Another occasion that has meant something to me is what is termed as an 'internal ADC.' I was lying on our settee one day in what I have already referred to as 'the twilight state' when I saw an image of my dad appear in my third eye, with my physical eyes closed. At the time I was not even thinking of him but saw an image of him sitting on a chair looking towards me; peering around a door. He was around twenty years younger than his final age and with a radiant smile on his face. He also had that moustache that he had in life that he never seemed to shave off.

When someone has touched your life with such kindness as my father did, it hurts you to see them in extreme physical pain before they pass away. When I had this experience it let me know all his pain and suffering had long since gone. He looked twenty years younger because when you leave the physical plane you can choose to be noticeable to others at an age you were most comfortable with. You also get a choice in how you are clothed in spirit. Some choose to wear their favourite attire whilst they inhabited the human form, others will feel more comfortable in robes. You still have choices.

Being able to tune yourself into your deceased family or friends you definitely need an open and trusting heart to start with. I liken it to playing the guitar because first and foremost the first thing you need to do is tune your guitar in before you even think of playing a tune. Once you are in tune you can't play a meaningful song straight away because it takes time, but with practice you learn and pick it up. In essence, you learn how to tune your ear into the inner workings of the spirit world too. It does take effort. It is certainly an explanation why sceptics will say that nothing has ever happened to them.

Another example is my wife who didn't want to have a 40th birthday party and was content just to be at home with her family to celebrate. Do you think that this would stop the spirit world coming to her? Not a chance as I am about to explain but first ask yourself this question. If you found yourself beside a body of clay that once was yours and realised you still existed, how would you try and communicate with your loved ones from then on when they can't see you? After all, it's not as if every front room around the world comes with a resident medium.

On her 40th birthday there was a hard rap on our computer, then a chair nearby made a noise like someone was trying to move it and next our kettle clanged, all within a second of each other. It was like someone ran through our lounge and kitchen hitting all three objects with a drumstick simultaneously. The message that we got from this was "Happy birthday from the spirit world." These are all subtle examples of messages that we should be looking out for.

I have personally been in someone's lounge who didn't acknowledge the spirit world but had lost their husband. All of a sudden during mid-conversation it sounded like someone was trying to move furniture around a few feet behind the settee, it was quite loud. I looked at everyone's faces around me and nobody even batted an eyelid. Considering it was a detached bungalow and everyone was accounted for in the room explained a lot to me. If it had happened in my house I would have been talking to it, even if it raised other people's eyebrows.

Another thing that happens in our house is if you are watching the television and an actor says "I love you" and you then hear a noise around you, like the countless ones I have already mentioned, then my understanding is that this is what the spirit world are letting you know. I always make a mental note of what was said before the noise because as I have said before the spirit world already knows the future.

The main purpose of our existence in the physical plane, that we currently inhabit, is to give love to others and as a consequence show that you are capable of being loved. If we cannot grasp this, in my honest opinion, we will keep coming back through reincarnation until we do so. There are many forms of life that are already grasping this and one of them is the animal kingdom.

As you would have picked up by now I am a self-confessed animal lover, especially of our canine friends. I was born (by choice) into a family that always had a dog and my first best friend was a small dog called Smartie. I loved him with all my heart. He would often appear out of nowhere, in the middle of town, and stand next to me as a toddler. My big sister Jane would then tell him to go home, which he obeyed. We idolised each other and I lost him in a heartbreaking way. My sense of loss as a small boy was immense. It was the first time in my life that I felt my soul ache. I still expect to be reunited with him one day because of the link of love.

This leads me to add more here. When my son was young he said that he saw another dog following our dog, Monty, around the house. He referred to it as being "The ghost Monty." We would retrace our steps and wonder why he made such a statement. The information that I gather from this is with my son's gift of seeing spirit (which eventually left him.) He was seeing animal spirits as well as human spirits. I should add that both Smartie and Monty were of the exact same build and stature. They were only coloured differently.

It has always been commented on how people love their pets and the pet loves them back unconditionally. I feel that we as humans often get carried away with what is deemed important. This could be the next holiday abroad, busy shopping trip, expensive electrical gadget, new car etc. We are often missing the point of being spiritual beings. Our happiness should be more geared to having food in the cupboards, clean water to drink, a warm home to live in and love and companionship in abundance. These are the important things that we truly cannot do without.

The show must go on

I would like to draw this chapter to a close and address a very delicate matter. When we are at the lowest ebb we can reach we may feel that there is no point to continue this life anymore.

We all have a different journey in life. We all have different things to put up with and to achieve, seldom are two examples the same. In a spiritual sense, our life is like a contract that we have agreed with the higher power. The only souls aware of this complete contract are your higher self, your guides and the higher power itself. To walk away from this life with the job unfinished is not meant to be the end result.

For instance, let me use myself as an example. I have had both significant highs and lows in my life; I have already shared many of them. If I had chosen to end my life before I interacted with students wanting to pass maths, then my actions would have a knock-on effect on other individuals. I believe in was destiny for me to meet them and help them in our journeys together, but then I effectively pull the rug from beneath them through my actions and affect their future as a consequence. I was able to break the subject down to a form that perhaps their school teachers either didn't have time to do individually or simply couldn't. If one person fails the subject, their future may run a different course because they do not have that certificate to prove their competence. I have then caused this to happen by simply not being there.

The message that I have received from reading a vast amount of books and seeing a multitude of live mediumship events, where suicide victims have returned to communicate, explains to me that in these circumstances souls are often extremely sorry. They are not only sorry to the people they leave behind but sorry for themselves for not completing their part of the deal.

However, we must remember that, although these individuals have taken themselves over, they do still exist and continue to have the same personality. The personality that was loved.

Chapter 17

There's no future without tears

There are quite simply times when some of life's best teachers (regardless of their age) don't get to stand and share their wisdom.

G.G.J.Sanders

There is that old cliché that you can choose your friends, but you can't choose your family. As I have already addressed from a spiritual standpoint this is not strictly true.

We have many experiences to go through in life so we can learn from them to continue soul growth. Sometimes, our extended family, who we are bound to fall out with on occasions, can teach us many things through good and bad experiences directly involving them. As a person that absolutely hates making mistakes I have learned not only from my own but also from others that have surrounded me since I was a child.

In retrospect, this makes us address obstacles in our life in a different manner. For example, if you were passed from pillar to post as a child it makes you want to be a constant in your child's life. If you attended a host of different schools it makes you want your children to have a more stable footing. If you were an only child you may want a large family in your future.

From my own experience of the distress of my parents' divorce when I was around five-years-old it made me realise that was not something I ever wanted my children to experience. Of course, a couple shouldn't be together if they are both miserable but marriage requires hard work, especially when children are part of that.

So does our higher self already know what is in store for us before we incarnate into our present life? Through my experience of finding out myself and it becoming a passion of mine since 12/10/2006 I would say a resounding "Yes." I often ask whether my once ten-year-old son knew all along to sit in a position behind the passenger and not the driver in that car accident so he could continue his life's journey. Was his soul given this information in advance?

I believe some part of our mind knows exactly what's coming up and, if it's not meant to be our fate, there may be intervention or attempted intervention of some kind. We can even help our own plight by keeping our ear firmly to the ground and listening to our sixth sense. All I can say from my own experiences is that if I have another experience like I did in chapter eight I will be ready to listen. Indeed, some authors will enlighten us with cases where ordinary people have given them outstanding evidence of divine help.

There are many questions I ask myself almost every day. Why did my best friend come to see me approximately two weeks before he died? I had not seen him previously for a couple of years before that. Why did I give him the only bear hug I had ever given him on the doorstep of my home that day despite not being a hugs type of guy? Why did he accept my story of paranormal activity in my house with a complete open mind? Why did he choose me to prove (to me) the continuation of the soul? I believe at the very least his spirit guides already knew and instructed him through his subconscious to visit me. Was my higher self also aware of all this coming up? I would never rule this out, we had our chance to say goodbye.

One of my early memories that involved my father that I have now relived several times, with hindsight, was when I had come back to my hometown to see him. We were outside the park, having just pulled over, in his car when I was around ten-years-old. As I reached for the lever to open the car door it felt like my hand was pushed off by an unseen force. Just as I failed to open the door a car came past at speed and I avoided my arm being attached to a flying door. Looking back I feel that this was not part of my life's path and something, most probably my guardian angel, intervened.

Approaching the middle of 2015, I met an old friend whom I had not had a meaningful conversation with for many years. After we asked what each other had been doing lately the floodgates seemed to open. I soon found out that one of his children had seen spirit when he was younger. Then came a story from my old friend that he could not really rationalise. I merely listened until he stopped talking.

As a contractor, he had been sent to an empty building to do some work with colleagues. As a tea break loomed, his colleagues went off for their break, but my friend wanted to push on with work. He walked towards a door that he knew was not locked but found he could not open it. After trying with a few shoulder barges and using all his might he simply gave up and then decided to catch-up with the tea break.

After the break had finished, he asked another man to try the door and it opened with ease. Just as the door opened, a beam came crashing down from high up towards the head of the man who had just opened it, but at the last second my friend with quick reflexes, pulled him out of the way. I soon gave my opinion that my friend's guardian angel had initially intervened saving his life. It simply wasn't his time to leave loved ones behind.

We largely associate bad things happening to good people in society because death is viewed as the final curtain. If you have thoughts of 'I have lost that wonderful person forever,' which was once my view, it offers no hope for us when we grieve loved ones. If you have my changed view of 'I will see them again and try not to torment myself,' life will get better and we can continue with more vigour.

Unfortunately, we cannot all make it to a ripe old age and die in our sleep. What I try to remember, with reincarnation in mind, is we are all here to have different experiences at different times. I often hear about a very poorly child that seemed to have such an understanding of their own ill health and address it in such a mature manner beyond their years. This can be deemed an 'old soul' (see my quote.)

Looking at things from a different angle, are we to believe that a child under five-years-old that watches something on TV with a theme tune, and then can go to their parents piano to play the tune note for note in its entirety, hasn't been here before? Or another child of a similar age that paints outstanding landscapes? Suddenly if you are familiar with life after death and reincarnation that light bulb moment happens.

The name you see on the front cover of this book is me, but it only represents my current experience. It represents this physical body that currently houses my soul. My soul has been known by many different names and has had numerable experiences. If I was regressed by the correct person, I believe that this could be unlocked. I strongly recommend reading 'Journey of Souls' by Michael Newton for a wider understanding.

For example, if it was unlocked that someone had lived ten different lives over 2500 years and had died in infancy twice, suddenly that saying 'only the good die young' doesn't quite have that sheer impact. Suddenly, the life of a relative of mine that did not survive infancy has created more understanding. I now ask the question who is in the better place? Is it myself or that wonderful child growing up in spirit?

It is my understanding that if we lead our lives with love, kindness and respect as core values, then we get to a place that is largely viewed by NDE's as paradise, or again by spiritualists as 'the Summerland'. It has been described as a place that has a warm sunny climate where we continue to do the things we currently do. A place with amazing colour where nobody gets ill and we no longer need sleep as we recognise it.

I was once in the audience observing who I would call a world class medium. I have seen this medium live numerous times, around half a dozen. When I spoke to him after my last visit, when he attended a local venue, he gave me advice on getting this book published after the show. I was merely a little cheeky and asked for some free advice. Remember, if you don't ask you don't get.

In the crowd on one occasion he directly picked out a young woman aged around twenty-years-old that he wanted to address. He told her that she should not feel guilty for the procedure that ended her unborn baby's life and that her grandmother was now raising the child in the spirit world.

The young woman let out a muffled shriek as if trying to cover her mouth before any sound came out and started to cry uncontrollably. He then came up to her chair and finished the conversation quietly with much compassion. What had happened was the child was unwanted and had been aborted, it had been addressed as a boy by the medium and now he was growing up in the spirit realms under the guidance of the relative.

What I noticed that day was after the initial tears there was such a relief and acceptance from the young woman. It appeared as though a weight had been lifted and soon after a gentle smile broke out across her face. The medium told her that the child knew what was going to happen before this life was chosen.

Not all souls are destined to walk this earth in every incarnation. I am strongly led to believe, from what I have learnt, that unborn babies can leave the womb spiritually whilst growing and know the future destined for them. This could be a potential reason for the baby being completely still for long periods and the mother getting very worried.

If you are going through hard times involving the harsh side of human nature try not to take things too personally; I speak from experience. We all go through these times. Sometimes the very important issues are how we deal with them and what type of character comes out the other side.

I can remember saving all my cash when I was a wide-eyed and eager teenager to get a lovely brand new red motorcycle helmet which was then stolen in a leisure centre a few weeks later. Then, I saved up for a better motorbike only to get forced off the road by a car and left for dead in a dyke. I was only on the road at that time to take my final payment to the person who had sold me the motorbike. I must have dropped about twenty feet from my initial sitting position on the road to the bottom of the dyke and could have been impaled by the handlebars. I will never forget thinking 'what could make a person do that to someone else as if their life meant nothing?'

If I had let moments like this and others consume me and affect how I interact with others I have found that I become the only loser. My firm belief is that those that have caused us distress will have to face their actions in their life review that is part of the akashic records.

What are the akashic records?

The akashic records (pronounced a-cash-ik) is a huge etheric library which contains every thought we have had, every spoken word that has crossed our lips and any action we have instructed our bodies to do since the beginning of time. Our current lives and what we did yesterday, for example, are already part of this library. It is like an ethereal CCTV system that never runs out of time or imagery for every person. Therefore, it also contains previous lives lived by us and the lessons we learnt before we incarnated again.

Can you imagine records that include every laugh, tear, moment of love, anger or cross word? What about an unpunished act such as a violent attack, murder, or something like an arson attack that remains only unpunished in our physical world through lack of physical evidence? The culprit then becomes unable to escape their actions; very powerful when you stop and give it some thought.

If you believe this as I do through my own 'flickering screen' experience and from what others are telling us through having a NDE it makes you want to continue to live an honest and giving life no matter what comes your way.

Sometimes I ask myself, "Why don't I always take the easy path and seem to choose the one with more rocks to fall over instead, but at the same time remain true to my heart?" Now I know the answer.

Chapter 18

Is it your loved ones paying a visit or is it something else?

There are many different circumstances that may cause a haunting, a spirit that seemingly gets stuck, regarded by some as 'an earthbound spirit.' A violent or sudden death can be examples. Sometimes the spirit refuses to move on until the full truth is known about the erroneous details of their passing, for instance, a murder that is covered up. Another example of 'an earthbound spirit' could be through materialism when the wealth generated in a lifetime is reluctantly left behind for others.

It is conceivable that the now discarnate individual will soon begin to realise that there is total accountability for all their actions in life. There may then be a total reluctance to move to an environment that represents their new home and so remain earthbound as a method of avoidance. A spirit could also be unaware that physical death has even occurred; I will give an example here.

Burt lives alone. He and his wife split up many years ago and his grown-up children, that he has a broken bond with, now live miles away. Burt has become bitter over time and he has had few meaningful relationships with people, he always viewed this as not his problem. He never remarried.

He thought that life after death was hogwash and it deserved ridicule. He had no time for entertaining conversation regarding it. One afternoon Burt had a huge pain in his chest and hit the floor hard soon afterwards. The thing was that Burt was back to his feet without remembering that he actually stood up; he felt no pain. In fact, it was the best he ever remembered feeling. All the aches and pains associated with old age were gone and he felt light.

Almost straight away there was a man in Burt's house (his guardian angel) that talked to Burt calmly and kindly. Burt wouldn't listen to this intruder and cut him short demanding that he remove himself forthwith from his house. The man did as requested as Burt refused to go away with him when instructed.

In a number of days, more people entered the house in high visibility jackets. Burt shouted at them to leave, but they didn't seem to notice his threats. When they left of their own accord Burt kicked at them with his foot. Burt has now become 'an earthbound spirit' as he is still attached to the physical plane and not attached to the spirit world.

Burt still lives in this house as he had done alone for years, but another family has now moved in. The family notice that something feels wrong and there is a cold chill in the house even in summer; the family often have bad dreams and their child reports of seeing an angry man that scares him. Other family members witness smells and loud noises although they see nothing. They have now put the property back on the market in their search for peace and quiet.

Whilst we are alive (in the physical sense) we all have choices. This doesn't change once we leave the physical as we still have the same personality and thought process. Here Burt had his chance but rudely sent someone trying to help him away. Some people who have had a NDE report to being collected like in this example. Certainly being hostile to others and not listening as well as you actually hear are not attributes of a particular personality.

Let me set up another scenario. A person that lives in a city with a heavy wartime influence reports to having seen soldiers walking through their property wall. These soldiers move as a normal group but don't seem to notice or interact with the owners. It is as if they are in their own little world.

Historically, this has been called 'the stone tape theory.' An event has occurred in history and this occurrence has been absorbed by the fabric of the building close to it and will replay the events seemingly at random like a tape recording. This can also be described as a 'residual energy.' The soldiers that were seen by the current owner of the property have long since moved on to the world of spirit. This replay of events once happened although many years ago.

If you have phenomena happening in your home, there are certain questions that you need to be asking yourself. Does it appear to be harmless, playful or does it thrive on your misfortune? Has a member of your family died regardless of whether they lived near you? Have you had renovations done to your property? Many questions, but once you establish answers to them you can build up a picture of what's happening in your environment.

The only time I have ever witnessed a spirit that thrived on my misfortune was when I went to a holiday property with my wife for a long weekend. We were kept up that first night by something running up and down the stairs and banging doors. The property was detached and what was meant to be a romantic weekend turned out to be very different with little sleep.

We were just talking about braving a second night when we heard what sounded like a wolf howl coming from inside of the property; not good. We packed and left within the hour and found that the property was built adjacent to an ancient burial ground. Whether it was one spirit or many I don't know, but as far as I am concerned it only takes one rotten apple to spoil the barrel.

There are sometimes issues with property renovations because spirits still have personality and know what they like and what they don't. This doesn't always coincide with the new owners choices.

On one occasion in my house, I started learning French from a CD. There I was oblivious to everything and on my own spurting out all the jargon when, all of a sudden, I had to repeat the French phrase for 'the bank,' which I can tell you sounds rather rude with an English ear. All of a sudden I heard laughter just over my right shoulder but as usual I was on my own in the house and could see nothing more than other human beings.

On analysis of this event I believe the laughter was from Mick, who had come to visit, and would have found the phrase very funny. It was right up his alley humour wise. There was no need to run out waving my hands in the air and calling for the exorcist. I was reassured that it was my best friend. It was harmless.

As I have said, our personality does not alter one iota when we stop breathing for the last time. However, if you go to bed one evening in your own home and sense something with you and it starts to make noise then tell it off. Explain that you are going to bed and have had enough of the day and want to sleep. You will be surprised how effective this is. The person that loved you still loves you and where you find love, you also find respect.

When we pass over and enter the light it does not mean that we cannot return to visit or comfort our loved ones. Sometimes when we lose someone we wrap ourselves up and shut ourselves away and all our hurt and pain stays with us. We won't let go of that person emotionally. This is not an isolated feeling but over time we need a back-up plan to make coping easier. My back-up plan was to visit a medium and embrace the spirit world.

If we refuse to let go we can tie the individual that we have lost to our hurt and pain. In essence, we are stopping them from moving on and continuing their journey, now in spirit. We always have things to do whether we have

133

a physical body or not. It's like stopping someone from going somewhere when they are just heading out of the door and changing their plans for them. Usually, they are not too happy about this.

Luckily there are very few examples of what I would term as a malevolent spirit, sometimes called 'a boggart' but they are quite easy to establish, they are driven by ill feeling. I would not necessarily put a poltergeist (noisy ghost/ spirit) into this category as I will soon explain.

Recently, I was talking about my shadow figure experience to someone I respected. This person then conveyed to me that he had known a family that had lost a child, a young adult. He stated that this person had died in significant pain, which put a tear in my eye when it was relayed to me.

What transpired was that many months after their death the mother and father awoke one night to hear a vast amount of noise in their front room downstairs. On venturing downstairs in a property that had always been their family home they noticed that there was no forcible entry but found that furniture had been moved around and stacked high. The front room that they left to go to bed had effectively been turned upside down.

This man telling the story then relayed to me that they called a clergyman to do a procedure to rid them of this boggart. When I heard this I was quite alarmed by it.

When we pass away we can be offered a spiritual sleep. I believe our taking of this sleep is often in relation to the way we died and our personality too. In a sense, the coma that we may have been in can be carried through to a hospital in the spirit world and we wake up when we are good and ready. The only thing is that when we wake up we find that there are no medical instruments needed to help make us better. They are simply not needed for a non-physical body.

I will relate this again to my best friend Mick. He was a strong ginger haired personality, whose hair later went whiter with age. He died tragically, but he was not one to sleep when it would have been offered. This may be why he came back within hours, sometimes referred to as a 'crisis apparition,' letting me know of the survival of the soul.

Mick had always been a lad that was up at the crack of dawn. He had a paper round that he loved doing and would disappear at about 5 AM on his BMX after I crashed at his house on a Saturday night. He also loved being half way down a river bank that ran through his village, holding a fishing rod. It always appeared to me that he had better things to do than sleep.

The only thing that made me a little jealous about Mick the personality was that he became such a good disco mover and all round entertainer that the girls liked him better than me. The fact that I considered myself better looking held nothing in real terms of how people seemed to flock around him. What did I learn from this? To do more work on my personality.

Now, back to the house turned upside down. In my honest opinion, their child had been away for many months of our physical time and had awoken from this sleep state and wanted to offer them this same evidence. My thinking is that they had little recognition for their subtle efforts in their old house over time so decided to do it 'big style.'

So my view is that this poltergeist or boggart, whichever view taken by them, was most probably their child just getting frustrated. I would not have used a priest but contacted my local spiritualist church and explained what was happening. A medium should then soon be in contact and anyone worth their salt would tell the family what was happening without any information at all about their family history. For me, it's all about ruling things out before a conclusion can be made.

I would like to bring this chapter to a close by talking about one of the most outstanding pieces of evidence of the continuation of the human soul that I have ever come across.

In 1919, a group photograph was taken of Goddard's Squadron which had served during World War 1, many men standing shoulder to shoulder. This photo that is widely available to be viewed online is now regarded as one of the greatest 'ghost' photographs of all time.

A face appeared in this photograph, in the back row, as if peeking over a colleague's shoulder, with a little wry smile on his face. It was recognised by the squadron as being Freddy Jackson. The only thing was that Freddy had been tragically killed two days prior to this photo being taken by an accident involving an airplane propeller. The day that this photo was taken was, in fact, the day of Freddy's funeral.

It is thought by many that Freddy was completely unaware of his death and just lined up like his colleagues for the shot to be taken. I go against the grain to this view and ask this question: why is he the only person on the photo seemingly peeking over someone's shoulder?

When you line up for a military photograph you simply would not get away with this lack of discipline. There would be a senior officer shouting at you to get in line properly. I put it to you that Freddy knew that he had died and had come back to attend his funeral and then line up with his friends.

One of the things I had found prior to finding this picture is that, when we pass away, not only are we given an option of attending our own funeral (if we are not in the sleep state) but also we are aware of the genuine and not so genuine thoughts (where applicable) of all the people that attend our funeral.

Although I don't know the full circumstances of this tragic accident involving the propeller, it would be logical to presume that Freddy suffered absolutely horrific injuries. The calm and unassuming look on Freddy's face, along with the fact that we shed the old overcoat (physical body) and are now provided with a perfect ethereal body speaks volumes.

It is my view that Freddy has merely returned to prove the continuation of the soul to the people who he respected. This is nothing different in real terms to my experience in chapter five with Mick. Freddy still had the same personality and thought processes, but now he had an ethereal body and got away with not standing shoulder to shoulder with his colleagues because nobody could see him with their physical eyes. The camera, however, did capture his spirit.

As with my experience with Mick, it is up to us whether we shrug our shoulders and immediately change the subject or jump up and down on the spot and run around telling people. For me, this is all part of being human.

Chapter 19

My answers to some questions

Only as my life unfolds before me, day after day, event after event, year after year, do I comprehend the magnitude of why I chose it.

G.G.J.Sanders

Q uestion) Why do some people seem to be coming forward to try to belittle mediums?

Answer) In the introduction, I mentioned that scepticism was the easiest option because it takes little or no effort. I feel it can say more about someone's frame of mind or personality, rather than anything else, to doubt without knowledge of a subject. There are those that want to look into things from another person's perspective and those that don't.

One of the recurring things I find is that because mediums are getting the correct information the sceptic will say that they are reading minds. That view seems defeatist to me as it's like sitting at a table with wobbly legs, for that statement doesn't hold any weight. I see their comments as a backhanded compliment because they have no other possible option to hold. In my sittings with mediums, I have found that they are actually tapping into a source. This is usually done clairvoyantly (including seeing spirit), using clairaudience (hearing spirit) or by using clairsentience (sensing spirit.)

If we play the devil's advocate and assume just for a minute that they are reading minds, then why are we as a society not utilizing their skills for jury service? Wouldn't a jury of psychic mediums work together better to get the correct decision in a court of law because of their unique gifts?

Q) What would you do in a situation where someone has wronged you and you cannot forgive them?

A) I merely talk out loud to my guardian angel explaining my situation and feelings and I ask for Karma to be restored. In other words, I am asking them to act in a way they see fit which leaves me to focus my interests positively. This often works.

Q) What would you say to someone who said that they find it hard to be nice because they themselves have been treated unfairly so many times?

A) It's the ultimate test of your character. All you can do in life is to offer your best and at least you know that you have been honest with yourself.

I believe it takes real strength of character to go through something unpleasant and still be nice. I would say don't let someone take your enthusiasm or energy from you. After all, this is often what they want, to take your smile away. If they do this then in theory they have won.

I remember miserable days at school because I let other people affect my happiness and I went home feeling rotten. Now I try to be happy around people that I feel don't like me. The thing to remember is if someone says something horrible to you they will probably forget within days, so why should you let it hurt you for years?

I have come across people that show signs of this 'passive-aggressive syndrome.' At the end of the day, it's their life which ultimately unknown to them becomes their life review. They will have to go through their actions in their life review and then seek forgiveness.

I have been in the audience of live mediumship events where a person has come back to beg forgiveness from someone seated. You will not be surprised to find out that the person seated is often extremely uncomfortable sharing what happened to them and the end result is a total reluctance to forgive the person's actions.

Q) What do you find frustrating about the things that have happened to you and others when you know that it is not your imagination?

A) Let's use the TV as an example. It's frustrating when we see a programme on the paranormal and they get someone who has never had your experiences to tell you that what has been experienced is something else. It's like watching a removal company giving advice on demolition work. For me, this just does not work.

Q) What would you say to someone that only accepts what science tells them?

A) Science, for me, is 'man made' in that it is devised by human beings to explain what is going on around them. It reflects our current (general) level of awareness and understanding. How would science explain a towel levitating in my home with no natural forces acting upon it? Science is more interested in matter and not spirit. However, it will continue to change as it has done in the past. New decades can create new understanding.

Q) Why do you think your best friend chose to come to you the evening he passed away and not another member of his family?

A) When Mick came to my house two weeks before his physical life ended we were talking about what we termed 'ghosts.' He already knew that I was a believer and we were best friends, which certainly would have influenced his mind that he took with him to the world of spirit.

There was a gap of just under five hours between his passing and me seeing him again. I believe that he was waiting for the correct moment in those few hours to make his appearance. I feel he picked the moment where I was unlikely to miss anything or run off because of the magnitude of the event. After all, how many people run for the hills when they have a paranormal experience when all alone?

It's important to clarify that Mick could have had his life review already in this five-hour time space because in the spirit world there is no concept of time. One week to them could literally be a heartbeat to us we just don't know. This could explain why some who have had a NDE report seeing a religious figure, there is more time involved to meet with the higher power than we give credit for.

Q) Do you feel that certain markers are put down in our lives for us to pick up on and then continue down a certain path with our future?

A) Yes, absolutely. When I was a young boy I had an unknown fascination with graveyards. I would stand near graves and quietly pay my respects in my mind to that person in the quiet peaceful surroundings. It sounds a strange thing for a young boy to do, but I have always been very sensitive and feel that this was one of my markers. I link it to the writing of this book.

Also, if we are born with certain strengths, for example, good with languages, cookery skills or being able to build something from scratch, then it seems very natural for us to follow these up in life and earn our living from them. However, when we grow with time other gifts, that we may even appear to stumble across, come to the front and may change our path.

Q) I lost someone that meant so much to me years ago. Do they know what I have achieved in my life since they have passed to spirit?

A) Yes. Our loved ones visit us like my maternal grandmother visits me. They can also become one of our spirit guides.

If there was a bond in life then there remains a bond. One thing to remember is your loving family member will know when there is a celebration around the family. For example, an engagement, birthday, wedding etc. Don't ever think they won't attend and observe what's going on. Raise a glass to them and celebrate the fact they are with you.

My maternal grandmother had never visited my house because she passed away before we purchased it, but she found us and knew where to visit when the old overcoat had been left behind.

Q) So what about my success? If I obtained my degree and made my fortune young would they be proud?

A) I have to say yes, but keep things in context. They would be proud of you because they love you, but in the great scheme of things, how much money you have and how many letters you have after your name often holds little importance in a spiritual sense. I remember getting my educational certificates framed and put on the wall, but soon took them down again because I thought it was too self-indulgent of me. We are viewed more by our nature and what we have done for humanity than what we achieve for ourselves. We are largely here to give of ourselves.

Relating this to my past, a cousin of mine came to me at a family get together (a while ago) and thanked me for once saving his life. I had forgotten about it, but then remembered dragging him out of a swimming pool coughing and spluttering when we were younger with the lifeguard looking in another direction. I'm not trying to portray a glossy or rosy picture of myself because, like anyone, I have made mistakes that I would prefer to change with hindsight.

Q) If my discarnate relatives love me so much then why have they not somehow given me the winning lottery numbers?

A) Looking at the bigger picture it probably was not your destiny for this lifetime. For example, if someone chose a lifetime to experience hardship then winning the lottery would be counterproductive to this experience and therefore nobody would be doing you any favours in handing you those magic numbers. You may have to come back again to obtain 'the hardship badge.'

Q) Do you think having a quiet environment is beneficial to having phenomena happen from your loved ones?

A) In ideal circumstances because some of the ways of communication need calm environments. One ADC I had a few weeks before my dad passed away was in the middle of the night when it was hot and my T-shirt had ridden up my back. I then felt a hand stroke my back twice during the night on the opposite side to where my wife was laying. This is another example of an ADC, it is called a 'tactile ADC.'

Q) Do you promote using Ouija boards to contact the spirit world?

A) I would never recommend using a Ouija board because you have no control over who you are summoning up. It can be very dangerous because you are inviting spirit communication at face value.

Q) It often haunts people when their loved one was involved in a fatal accident and they worry about the pain that they must have been in. Can you shed some light on this?

A) Often we associate pain when there was none involved. I have read that angels have the power to remove your soul from your physical body before an impact when they know you stood no chance of survival. I believe this with all my heart.

Q) What about a disaster where a person has been in a fire or been in a building that has been flattened, what happens to the real us?

A) The real you that is your ethereal body (your soul) cannot be destroyed. Flames and buildings collapsing happen in our physical world. Your ethereal body is not physical and, therefore, cannot be damaged. I refer you back to the story of Freddy Jackson in the previous chapter.

Q) Do you maintain that things happen for a reason?

A) I feel very strongly that they do. I could go into many things that have happened to me both good and bad and it is only with hindsight that I discover why they have happened to me. One of the most recent in my life is that I have never had a healthy bank balance and it was not until I was involved in a car accident, that was not my fault, that I then realised I could take things further and not only write this book but get it published too.

Q) Can you give an example of times you may have felt your spirit guides close to you?

A) The times that come to mind most are in group meditation (see the next chapter) or funnily enough in the bathroom in the early hours of the morning when I visit. The times I have heard a significant loud noise around me are too numerable to mention; like the rattling of the bath panel. I nearly jump out of my skin when this happens. The spirit world appears to have a knack of making things happen when water is close by. After all, it is one of those natural elements that appears to have been around since the beginning of time. Remember Mick came through the wall when water pipes were on the other side of it.

Also, when someone in our household is genuinely sick, the spirit noises associated with our house can be significantly amplified.

Q) You talk about the silver cord that is attached to our physical body. Do you think that you have ever felt yours?

A) Yes. For instance, when I connect with a beautiful song I will say I feel the tug of the silver cord. More about this coming up in a later chapter.

Q) What other ways will my loved ones in spirit give signs of being around me?

A) A classic example is the moving of objects such as ornaments, pictures or car keys. The person affected by this phenomenon will usually not see the moving of the objects but just knows they didn't leave them in that place.

Q) I often hear people talk about white feathers and them being placed by angels for the correct person to find. What are your views?

A) I have had my own experiences of this and can confirm the answer is "Yes." However, you need to use a little common sense in how they are found. If you have a pillow case and see a white feather next to it you should probably take it with a pinch of salt.

My most memorable white feather find was a few hours before my father passed away when I saw a white feather in mid-air, motionless, as if being held out for me by an invisible hand. I looked around to try and find the meaning, held out my hand and took it inside with me. I feel an angel was offering me solace, letting me know my dad was being looked after as he entered his final hours. Of course, I didn't find this out until later.

Other times I have prayed at home about something and found a white feather outside my back door which was stuck to the ground with something glue like. My interpretation of this is "We got your message."

Q) What is your explanation for people having bad dreams?

A) One explanation is that when we are asleep we often visit the astral plane. As there are different layers of this astral plane we don't always connect with the right one and so we end up in the wrong place. I liken it to an innocent child walking out into the big world without a parent beside them. It can sometimes get scary and we can end up in a place we weren't meant to be in.

Q) If there are different levels of the astral plane can everybody move about to a different plane of existence if they choose?

A) I have read many books on this and the resounding opinion is that you are allowed to come down from a more advanced level but you are not permitted to move up unless you advance spiritually.

Q) Can you say what your relationship is with the divine?

A) It isn't anything generic that is written by another's hand. It is like having a healthy relationship with a dear friend. I can only explain this as if you have two friends and one of them has a wicked sense of humour; the other being very serious about everything. You wouldn't tell them both your best joke. If I did that I would have a generic relationship with them. We are all individuals and don't have to pretend to be something that we are not as long as we are not being offensive.

Q) What ratio of males to females do you find in a typical mediumship event and why do you think this is?

A) I would say that there are seldom cases where the audience is more that 15% male. When a medium has pushed and asked a random male why they are in the audience, you will often get a reply of being dragged in by a spouse. In my opinion women are naturally more sensitive than men. So when you get a male sceptic brought in on a television programme I often have a laugh out loud moment.

I do think that the typical male thought is that someone is trying to dupe them 'with all of this nonsense' and they feel 'too clever' to be fooled.

Q) You seem to have an affinity with the learning disability group. How would you advise a person that has never interacted with them to approach them?

A) With a warm smile, kindness and a genuine interest in what they are doing, that's it really. I have found they much prefer animated people who will acknowledge them as an individual, almost in as much as children who have their favourite grandparents who are the most fun to be around. I always communicate with respect like I would with any other adult, but I try my best to be fun around them. They as a group are often connected to their inner child and so am I, so it works perfectly.

Also, there are too many broken promises and empty gestures in life that we have all witnessed. If you want someone to see you as a role model you go to the other end of the scale and they see you for who you are.

Q) You talk about your life turning full circle, from when you were fourteen-years-old, in terms of being with the learning disability group. Do you feel this was part of your life's plan and you lost the correct path?

A) I believe if you are not on the correct path things will happen to get you back there. My true path had in fact been the initial one. You could say I had just not taken the time to listen to my heart.

Q) Do birthmarks have a spiritual significance?

A) They can represent scars from previous lives and possibly how we died. There is a member of my family that had a birthmark on one side of their abdomen and a clear birthmark on the other side, like an entrance and exit wound that could have been caused by a sword or a bullet.

Q) Do you think it was your destiny to write this book?

A) Yes, I am a person who likes to give. I feel that I am giving hope to people who have loved and lost and it would be an injustice to keep this information to myself.

Often, when I have sat at my computer and worked on the chapters that you currently see before you the spirit noises in my house go off simultaneously like a firecracker in my immediate environment. I see this as encouragement from my discarnate loved ones and spirit guides.

Q) Why did you effectively go solo with this book and not hand everything over to an established major publishing agent?

A) The best way I can answer this question is this: as you know from reading previous chapters, one of my rare natural gifts (we all have them) is to do impressions of characters. Apart from the ones already mentioned, I can do certain Little Britain characters and also ones from the Austin Powers movie.

A few years ago I decided that I wanted people to be aware of what I could do and approached around thirty agencies asking them if I could send them evidence of this. Only one agency got back to me.

After a few days, I had given them evidence of what I was capable of only for them to tell me that they enjoyed what I had given them, but they thought it was best for me to come in and attend what was like a group seminar. This would cost me hundreds of pounds that I didn't have. You see the pattern here, they effectively wanted my money. I then asked myself this question "Who was going to gain from this experience?"

My view with this book became that I didn't need someone knocking me back or saying "No," when I knew in my heart that I had something worthwhile. If you are honest with yourself (and your own worst critic at the same time) but you still feel a desire to proceed, then why should someone else stop you in your tracks. They don't share your passion.

I knew that I had a compelling story to share which was surrounded in truth. I have found a recurring theme with certain famous people. They were continually being knocked back because nobody wanted to entertain them. Only sheer belief in what you are capable of achieving seems to win through. One of my beliefs is that if you don't respect yourself how can you expect others to respect you?

Chapter 20

Mind reading?
What about this!

Mediums are often questioned when, in fact, what they have is a natural gift. On the other hand we never seem to question when a young person picks up a musical instrument and starts playing it like a grandmaster.

G.G.J.Sanders

In October 2012, I went to something called a psychic supper where you pay a fee and get a reading from a psychic medium with your supper thrown in too. It was a themed charity event and the first time I had been to one. I knew something was going to happen that was memorable when I felt something touch my head just as I was going to get a soft drink. I immediately looked around and nobody was there. I should have known better than to even try to reason in a physical sense. It was like someone patting a dog as if to say "Good boy," I just knew that this was where I was meant to be at this stage of my life.

I soon saw a lady who beckoned me to approach her from our table; it looked like I was to go first. I was the one nearest to her after we had sat in random places. There were eight people on our table, but the hall was packed as we all got ready for our fish and chips to be cooked in the licenced premises across the road. In fact, I had never seen so many different mediums in such a confined space.

The lady that beckoned me over was called Susan Hind; I had never seen or heard of her before, but she was local. In time, I was to find out she was a Psychic Medium and Healer. She then sat me down and, with a closing of her eyes and a little shake of her head from left to right, started to open up and relay some things to me about how she perceived my personality and issues in my life (with her warm sunny nature.) She then reeled off fourteen facts about me one after the other like she had been my twin sister. I found my jaw loosening minute after minute the more she talked.

These fourteen facts were not at all like you are married and have children, this was too easy. She started with, "I have your maternal grandmother here and she wants to give you something." Firstly, I must convey my maternal grandmother shows up every time I see a medium. I have never had contact from either of my grandfathers or my other grandmother since I have been seeing mediums, which started around the year 2001. The medium will always convey that it is my mother's mother. For me, the link has been a true and unbroken bond of love from her.

However, the issue of wanting to give me something was a bit of a sore point. My grandmother had over twenty grandchildren and for some reason, that only she could explain, decided to give only money to one grandchild in her will. Although I would not describe myself as a person driven by money, it still hurt me when I found out her wishes. All I wanted was to be treated equally, no more, no less. This point coming from Sue reinforced to me that the spirit world do know our thoughts and can feel our pain or anguish.

Other points were then delivered thick and fast. For instance, Sue knew that I had been clearing up in my garden in the last forty-eight hours and said that my grandmother was there watching me do it; taking into account that it was in fact October. Another breathtaking fact she mentioned was that when I put pegs on the line to hang out the washing (remember I'm a bloke here for starters) she said that I went by colour sequence. For instance, I would use blue pegs then red pegs and then green pegs rather than pick up random colours. Everything Sue was saying to me was 100% accurate.

Other facts were that someone in the family had a birthday that was imminent, which was my daughter and likewise for someone seeing an optician, which was me. I was told that I was very quick at crunching numbers and my thought process was not superficial. She also mentioned that I didn't suffer fools gladly and that I would be a kind boss employing well-deserved people. My rule of thumb in management would be employ by personality or kindness before qualifications. This is a view that seems to be getting more commonplace. Without human kindness around you can be a poor environment to be in. I have witnessed this first hand.

After that evening, I felt compelled to go and see Sue again at a future date. I had found someone who appeared to know their profession back-to-front and I didn't want to let go of finding a psychic medium of this quality. I can only explain this like if you find a good plumber or electrician you would be foolhardy to try another when you have seen first-hand what that person in front of you is capable of. For me, it is a case of sit and wait until they can fit you into their schedule if you can, be patient. I must say there certainly is never any pressure put on you to see anyone again and that is how my session ended, Sue didn't ask for my name and I didn't give it either.

When I saw Sue a few months later she started to talk about my maternal grandmother again. Considering my grandmother had lived in the same town as my father and I had left the area as a five-year-old, there certainly was lots about her that I didn't know. I awaited information with keen interest. Sue mentioned that it was being impressed on her that my grandmother's middle name was Mary. I told Sue I had no idea of this information. A few seconds later Sue told me that she used to use 'Lily of the Valley' perfume too, again I had no idea. Other facts that I could confirm were as usual highly accurate.

That night after I had time to digest everything I felt compelled to phone my uncle Paul who was my grandmother's first born son. He confirmed straight away that her middle name was indeed Mary and she used that very perfume that Sue had mentioned. I would put it to any sceptic who believes that mediums read minds; how could she be reading my mind when the information had never been there for her to retrieve?

At the end of this reading, Sue gave me the option of attending her circle. In a nutshell, I would be surrounded by a small group of like-minded people once a week.

There is a spiritual law that says 'like attracts like.' The more I have reflected on this saying over the years the more it has come back time and time again to prove itself to me. How can you explain this law in a nutshell? Well, someone that viewed himself as a man's man is unlikely to have a best friend regarded as a family man. A charity worker is unlikely to have a close friend who camps himself in the bookmakers every day looking for a deposit on a brand new sports car and so on.

I always remember overhearing a lady once say "You get the husband that you deserve." Although there are always exceptions to a rule, this is a general phrase that is a good example of 'like attracts like.'

In the circle that I was soon to attend for the first time, we would be saying a short prayer, meditating and having a go at various things like reading from specialized cards and psychometry. Psychometry being the holding of an object, for example, a ring or watch and then you give information about the possible discarnate person that once owned it.

For a person that had minimal experience of how to meditate, I can tell you that group meditation is quite a powerful experience. You are collectively there with your spirit guides present. At times, the energy in the background of this quiet room sounds like a firecracker of noise going off around you, like an electrical charge in the air.

I feel it is important to have a trained medium with you and I wouldn't sit in a group without one. When I sit there and meditate in a group one of my first thoughts is always my happy journeys with my learning disability group. Imagine all those guardian angels present in the same place listening to all that happy conversation and laugh out loud moments on the minibus, it never fails to put a smile on my face.

I have found that I have strengths and weaknesses in the group circle, but I have already started to develop some clairaudience. I can only describe this personally as meditating so deeply that you hear a voice telling you things. The voice sounds like that internal stereo system that I have previously described. My experience of it is more of a monotone effect, there are no peaks and no troughs, but the voice is clear, constant, soothing but also a little quiet.

Then when you get information the important thing is to remember it word for word and relate the information to the group. I have been given names relating to other members of the circle's family and friends and how they passed to spirit. I have also found out from my meditating in the group that one of my guides is called Starc, so now I know who to address when things in life trouble me.

With this in mind, it really makes me wonder when vulnerable people relay to 'professionals' about hearing voices and can then be (depending on the individual case) given high amounts of medication and sometimes institutionalised. This is another thing in life that makes me shudder the more I think about it when many have no belief in anything outside our five senses.

The more conversations you have with like-minded people, the more you have in common with them and the more open you can be regarding your experiences. There always seems to be total acceptance from the group when you relay an event that has happened in your life regardless of how bizarre it sounds.

There are many reasons for people sitting in a regular circle. There would be no way I would have chosen this environment without all the happenings in our house or that visit from Mick at my work that night. Some of the reasons for the other members of our circle attending are even more profound than my own. I am not allowed to share these unfortunately as one of the golden rules of our group that Sue says on a regular basis is, "What happens in the circle stays in the circle" and quite right too.

One thing I was soon to find out that I had in common with Sue was we had both been that child that liked to stand in front of graves and quietly pay their respects in thought that I have already relayed. For me, it was more evidence that every soul that walks the earth has a path destined for them and markers are put down for us to follow. One of Sue's markers was to give one to one evidence of the afterlife, effectively working for spirit. And mine is working for spirit, but coming from a slightly different angle; with the publication of this book.

In a more recent communication with Sue, she started talking about my father in spirit. She then gave me an important date my father wanted me to know, given as the March 10th. I could not find any relevance to this date but knew with Sue I could trust the information. On the way back home I must have said this date to myself twenty times so that I could check my list of important family dates that I had. As soon as I stepped through the front door my wife handed me the telephone, it would have to wait.

My uncle Robin was on the other end of the line. Robin was my maternal grandmother's last born child. He was the last of seven children; being the sixth boy. We shared a mutual love of cricket and football and could probably bore our spouses to death talking about these sports. I had not been in contact with Robin for months and I was the one that would usually ring him.

When the conversation finished about half an hour later, I got back to looking up that date given and found March 10th was, in fact, my uncle Robin's birthday. I believe my father was telling me that my uncle was about to ring me. Remember the spirit world knows our future.

Chapter 21

Let your actions of today move other souls

If someone is not interested in my kindness when it is offered I soon begin to realise it's not the kindness that's wrong, I've just been offering it to the wrong person.

G.G.J.Sanders

Another scenario, Tim is going for an interview. He has prepared himself like the meticulous individual he is. A bright young man, he has got all his certificates ready, wearing his best suit and has looked up the company and done his research knowing virtually all there is to know about how they operate. He is clued up and very confident he will get the job.

However, after answering a number of questions positively he is asked what is the nicest thing that he has done for a complete stranger? This catches Tim on the back foot and he fumbles for his words because he hasn't got an answer. He asks for the question to be brought up again near the end of the interview so he can give it more thought, but his confidence has been affected. As a perfectionist, he wanted everything to follow a pattern.

At the end of the interview the manager asks Tim to point out his car in the car park and then relayed to Tim that he felt he could tell a lot about an individual by the way they drive their car. Tim looks back very puzzled.

He then tells Tim that he had a dental appointment that very morning and was following Tim for a few miles up to the offices. He gives various pointers on how he perceived him from the journey including the driving over a zebra crossing when there were people waiting to cross, driving through a red light and ignoring right of way when he should have waited for another car coming towards him. The job was not offered to Tim.

I am going to stick my neck out here and say that kindness seems to be in short supply in this world. Kindness is a thing that can be shown in the easiest of ways or the smallest of gestures and this includes whilst we are driving. For example, some drivers treat you like if they let you out into the traffic it is like they are giving away their last twenty-pound note. There will be the closing up of space, the tightening of their grip on the steering wheel and a reluctance to look in your direction when they have effectively blocked your route completely. This can happen to any driver even when you are transporting vulnerable individuals.

In society there appears to be a concentration on money; getting a pile and watching it grow. Important issues can then be overlooked like having tunnel vision. I have witnessed this particularly with one company I used to work for. There was so much attention paid to profit margins that the small but still highly important things were grossly overlooked and I was embarrassed to work for the company. You may also get the impression that the company feels it owns you like the fixtures and fittings to add to the equation and boy don't they get irritable if you get sick!

I have heard it said that if you notice a fault in yourself, it is more meaningful than spotting a multitude in another person. Indeed, this logic once helped me to get a job. In the middle of an interview I was asked to name three of my known faults, I immediately asked for the question to be brought up again at the end of the interview so I could give it more thought. After many more minutes, the interviewer forgot all about it and as I was about to get up and go I brought up the subject again. I then relayed three things that I felt needed improving on that would not have harmed my chances of getting the job.

An hour later the phone rang and I was offered it. My immediate thought was 'how many of the other candidates openly admitted that they had things to address without taking things personally, effectively ruling themselves out of the running?'

I would now like to relate to you the nicest thing a complete stranger has ever done for me. Many years ago I was driving my car low on fuel, with Allison by my side, and we broke down with no fuel left. I looked around and saw a young man, roughly my age, doing something to a car in the distance. As I approached him we smiled at each other and then I asked him if he could help. He then got a long rubber tube and a container and literally sucked the fuel out until it started to come from his car.

When there was enough fuel to get me to the next garage he stopped and handed me the container and refused to take any money off of me despite me pestering him to do so. As I approached my car I looked back one last time to admire the person who had helped me in need. I then saw him spitting out petrol that had gone into his mouth. He had waited until I walked away to do this and I felt absolutely rotten for what my actions had caused. I also thought what a best friend he would make somebody as my eyes genuinely welled up a little.

In fact, that day taught me one of life's lessons in that if you do something for someone else, especially if you don't know them from Adam, it can be a very uplifting moment in your life.

Now I would like to flip the coin and relate some of the things I have done for strangers in my recent history that I didn't know. If you feel that I am merely blowing my own trumpet please feel free to skip to the next chapter.

My take on life is that I can't change the world but what I can do is influence my immediate surroundings wherever I go. I can do this through my home life, my work and when I'm mixing with others whilst out and about. I very much agree that we should treat others as we would want to be treated, if I see others that refuse to do this it isn't my job to change them, but it is my job to still expect the best out of myself.

Kindness is similar to love. If you, as a person, don't give it out you are very unlikely to get it back.

I remember seeing a blind woman and her guide dog coming to a halt on the pavement, in front of them was an empty van blocking their way. The dog knew what was expected and refused to budge from the spot because, if it did, it would be amongst the moving traffic. I saw the blind woman's look of total confusion on her face as she came to that halt. She had no idea why her dog had refused to move any further.

With people just driving past something inside of me told me that this was simply not good enough and that I must offer my services to the situation. Within minutes the problem was solved, I had served my purpose. I watched them walk off together on the other side of the van. When I do something like this it feels like someone has given me something, I feel a buzz like my soul is connecting with something. I wanted to give the van driver my thoughts on his actions but experience has taught me not to put myself in these positions, after all, a compromise had been reached.

I can relay that many people regret times when they could have helped in a situation when they have a NDE and get to see their actions replayed to them from what already forms the akashic records. In a nutshell, if we as a society reorganised our priorities a little more we would soon realise that we are here to give our time and consideration to others. It should not take a huge spiritual event to realise this.

One of the things I have learnt, especially from some difficult secondary school days, is if you are offended by very little then you hold little resentment. Bullies, for example, usually pick on gentle souls that offer little resistance and they get a kick out of seeing you miserable. I now try to forgive others immediately so I can stay positive for others.

On another occasion, I saw an old man leaning up against a post and panting hard. I pulled over and asked him if he needed my help. I found out he was a ninety-eight-year old who then told me he was exercising. He mentioned that he walked for a while and then rested because he felt that if he gave up on exercise, he would soon perish. The vibe I got from him was either that he loved life or indeed he was scared of dying, possibly both. He thanked me for being concerned as I said goodbye and walked away.

The last story I would like to leave you with is when I went to a local freezer centre. There was a guy doing his shopping on his own with so many plastic tubes around his person my immediate thought was that he may have cancer. All of a sudden another customer nearby informed him that his large milk had leaked all across the whole shop floor. As he looked at the milk, his head sank and looked like he could cry at any moment. I moved in and told him to give the milk to the person at the till and I would get him a fresh one from the other side of the store. A couple of minutes later a concerned face looked more cheerful again. In fact, the lady who had told him of the leaky milk looked at me with an expression of 'what are you getting from this?' I most probably looked back with a glint of 'I know something you don't know.'

I can assure you that when I get to look back on my life one day when disconnected from my physical body, I want to look back with pride and not regret. My soul is always learning lessons intended for it (for soul growth.) After all, it is why I am here in the first place.

The power

If we let someone upset us then we are handing over the power. The power of whether we have our next smile, laugh or we embrace the next person who deserves comfort.
Keep the power, show them your strength and wear the smile of kindness in your life because kindness is always a strength.

G.G.J.Sanders

Chapter 22

Soul mates & soul time

Your soul mate may not have a brand new car or be able to shower you with gifts but the chances are they will not only understand you more than anyone else but cherish you too because you're unique.

G.G.J.Sanders

Y ou will rarely find an author describing soul mates that will not make a connection to reincarnation and us living previous lives with them. Some that are new to this subject may get the vibe that soul mates are linked to us by romance and romance alone. This view, of course, is incorrect as there are different types of soul mate. A soul mate is someone that we have a deep rooted connection with, that is in our lives or yet to be in our life, for a given purpose.

My rule of thumb for assessing if I think a person is a soul mate is the pull of my heart strings when I imagine time away from them or indeed no longer have them in my life. This soul mate could be a parent, grandparent, sibling/twin, uncle or aunt, cousin, friend, lover and so on. Sometimes there is friction involved with a soul mate because lessons need to be learned for our soul growth. Don't expect just one soul mate per lifetime because you may have many.

The romantic in all of us will want to find the soul mate that is commonly known as the 'eternal flame' soul mate. This is that special someone that makes us feel complete, like two halves that form to make a perfect whole. There should never be any fear from each other and awkward silent moments aren't part of the connection. 'Eternal flame' soul mates are seldom to do with sheer passion between two people because passion can fizzle out rather quickly. You need common ground.

One thing that puts fire in my belly is when a relative, friend or acquaintance will approach you and tell you that they feel that you are with the wrong person. Yes, I have had this happen to me. It is quite insulting when someone is trying to match you with someone else when you know in your heart that your search has already ended. In essence, they are trying to tell you that they know you better than you know yourself. My advice is not to be told that someone knows who your soul mate should be better than yourself; after all they are not living your life on your behalf.

We don't always share the same physical lives with our 'eternal flame' because of the learning lessons element of our individual journeys. When I think of my father and the lack of luck he had in love I truly hope that his 'eternal flame' soul mate was waiting for him when his journey was complete. I believe he really did deserve that unconditional love that he never seemed to find in his life.

It's hard to envisage, but a relative of ours in this incarnation could have been a romantic link to us in a previous life. I often relay to my wife that I would much prefer us to have a platonic sibling relationship in a future life rather than never being linked again. This is another angle for soul mates.

I certainly do feel that certain soul mates come into our life to teach us a lesson and then for some reason make a retreat maybe through a fall out that can't be reconciled or even death. Was Mick a soul mate? I certainly feel he was. He taught me how to express myself through words, actions and humour like no other. He had an established personality and sense of humour and could very well have been an 'old soul.'

So how do you find a soul mate that has not entered your life yet? Well, I feel that we should always keep our eyes and ears open. Our spirit guides are often planting things in our grey matter for us to pick up on. For instance, have you ever gone out of your front door and been reminded of something really important that had huge implications when your thoughts were miles away? Was it you who remembered or did the idea get planted there?

The unrealised soul mate could even be that person that has been in your local supermarket the last four times you have been in there and you know you're not being followed because they were there first. Why were you both in there together every time, coincidence? I no longer believe in coincidences.

Find an excuse to talk to this person rather than just pass trolleys again feeling uncomfortable. Maybe you should accidently (on purpose) drop a packet of something in front of them so they have to stop and you can start a conversation by apologising for being clumsy. I once heard a story where a person used their mutual love of dogs to attract their soul mate and it was a mixture of careful planning and dog work that got them together. Never take the easy option of not making any effort.

What about the married couple who look back on their lives and realise that they were in the same photograph as children despite being in different family groups? My wife, for instance, lived less than a mile away from me for five years until we introduced ourselves. How many times did our paths cross in this time despite never knowing each other? After all, you never talk at length to a person whom you are unfamiliar with.

When she did come into my house for the very first time, as teenagers, she told me that she had already played in my front garden as a child. She had done this many times before I actually lived there. Could it be our guides getting us ready for us to meet?

Hanging out with your soul

In a physical world that seems to not have much space left it feels good just to create a little time and hang out with number one. Sometimes it's hard just to give yourself some time in your own schedule. It's good just to hang out with yourself, like going for a jog, swimming, meditating, fishing, gardening, reading, or even things that involve an animal soul too like walking the dog or horse riding. Make sure that your mobile phone is switched off for a short while.

Three of my favourite examples of hanging out with my soul are when I walk my dog, lock the bathroom door to have a shower or listen to soothing music. In fact, some of my best moments of thought, that I feel the divine helps with, come when I am in a field somewhere with my canine friend beside me or indeed under running water.

However, I have to admit that listening to a wonderful song (often in the form of a ballad) is something that truly connects me with my soul. When I hear that special song, that always seems to choose me, it makes hairs stand to attention and in listening (with some volume) I honestly can feel that tug of that silver cord lifting my soul. Often I feel cleansed and buzzing afterwards rather than depressed as some may think. After all you either feel the vibe or you don't. I am a firm believer that tears can cleanse the soul.

Life, for me, is about searching and I have searched for years to find this collection of songs. So here they are, friends to my soul; they might just give you shivers too. There is not one song listed here that has not put a tear in my eye or sent cold shivers down my spine.

Confunkshun:	Let me put love on your mind.
Taylor Dayne:	Love will lead you back.
Andrea Bocelli:	Because we believe.
Oleta Adams:	I just had to hear your voice.
Michael Buble:	At this moment.
Shayne Ward:	Over the rainbow.
Celine Dion:	All by myself.
King's of Leon:	On the chin.
Chris De Burgh:	Songbird.
Bobby Womack:	Someday we'll all be free.
Stylistics:	Thank you baby.
The Beatles:	Something.
Charlie Wilson:	My favourite part of you.
Paul Johnson:	Half a world away.
Black:	This is life.
Kut Klose/Keith Sweat:	Get up on it.
Foreigner:	That was yesterday.
Lighthouse Family:	Lost in space.
Rumer:	Slow.
Chicago:	Hard habit to break.
Gregory Abbott:	I'll find a way.
Tears for Fears:	Memories fade.
Teddy Pendergrass:	All I need is you.
Kurt Nilsen:	Before you leave.
Whitney Houston:	You give good love.

When I got married it was not as easy as it is now to search and find a great song because technology has moved on. As a result we kind of settled for 'our song' on the day being good rather than outstanding. I believe too many people have a wedding song that is too mainstream. I was guilty of this myself. If I had known the song 'All I need is you' by Teddy Pendergrass actually existed then it would have been our wedding song as it is the one song that truly captivates everything I have ever felt for my wife.

I feel the one thing that encapsulates all these songs is the outstanding performance by the singers involved. It is as if when they finished the vocal performance they needed an hour to lie down in a darkened room to compose themselves once more. They are all incredible performances.

Chapter 23

The final curtain,
when the veil is lifted

A s we know, life is precious and can be extremely delicate. When we start off in the world as a baby we are very vulnerable and reliant on others for our every need. When the coin is flipped and we look at the elderly and infirm we see (in some cases) that things are repeated. There can be the heavy reliance on others, the inability to control bodily functions, struggling to make people aware of what we want and waiting for your next drink or meal to be presented to you.

As you would have gathered from early in this book I am totally convinced that certain children can see spirit, both my children have. I was a father in my early twenties. So when, before any of my personal experiences started, and my mother beckoned me over to tell me that my daughter had seen another child in her house and introduced herself to my daughter as 'Emily,' I was dumbfounded.

I feel children see spirits because they have recently come from spirit themselves. I find that young children are extremely honest and will talk about any subject with a matter of fact nature. Do you think they won't bring your bad habits to your attention? Many years ago my young daughter often told her grandfather, Roy, to have a wash and shave. He would do this almost straight away and then presented himself back in the room for a comment of "That's better granddad."

There is no reason for small children to make things up. They have little to gain from being deceitful and have come from a place governed by thought, where you are unable to hide what you think. There is not much at a young age to cloud their minds like we have, and as a consequence they seem more aware of spiritual matters.

Imagine a child going to an adult and talking about a person that they have seen, only for the adult to treat them like they have done something wrong. This can be a reality of the event. Even mediums have had childhoods where their parents or a member of the extended family have hushed them up quickly and told them never to repeat what they have said. There may even have been a clip around the ear to go with it.

Children can see spirit up to a certain age. So what is this age? Of course, it will vary, but you find that the vast majority are said to stop seeing spirit by the age of puberty. If you have a child that has an imaginary friend, for example, I would say to you that imagination has nothing to do with it. This person exists but not in the way that we do, it's just that we adults can't see them.

Imaginary friends will often show themselves to the child in communities where there is little or no interaction with other children. They could be the first child in the family, for example. I believe the spirit world often arrange this so there is reduced isolation or loneliness. Here, the first born child will get to interact with someone else, despite us not seeing them.

You will notice in the vast majority of cases that it is water off the duck's back to the child who interacts with the spirit world because they don't seem to differentiate between the two worlds. My advice is to take it seriously and never stop asking questions. This imaginary friend could be a distant relative not only looking out for the welfare of the child concerned but your welfare too. Maybe looking at old family photographs with the child may bring up more than you could ever imagine.

Like I have already addressed, we can revert back to being childlike when approaching the twilight of our lives. At the very end of our lives, particularly if we have a long illness, things can again change back. What I am saying here is we again become aware of spirit because the transition is about to take place again, we are going back to spirit.

As soon as we are born we are all soaking up information from various sources which eventually will make us the personality we are today with all our views. The information that I have found since my life changing experience has shown me that dying people's behaviour and comments will often have others around them scratching their heads. Relatives around the scene will not know what to say and some may talk to the person in a condescending manner as if they don't know what they are talking about and try and change the subject quickly. The chances are that the person at the end of their life will then become even more frustrated when the issues raised are rebuffed.

As you may remember from an earlier chapter, observations were made around my father-in-law, Roy, where he looked at a point in the room and started to smile before he slipped away. Was this a loving member of his family, from spirit, coming to collect him? Or even a group of people? Now I have opened my mind, I certainly believe so.

Often the language coming from the person lying in bed will be about making a journey to a new place. They may use language which involves getting on transport or having their suitcase ready for a trip. After all, if you see (and hear) someone you love who informs you that you are about to go on a surprise journey with them what would your topic of conversation be?

There may also be a complete change in the person's mobility and they will sit themselves up even though they had not been able to move for days before this. They may themselves act as an intermediary between other family members who have already passed to spirit and then relay information to family around their bed. The family around the bed may think that the loved one at the end of their life is seemingly getting better, only for them to slip away shortly after the burst of energy and communication from the other side.

There have been accounts of conversations between the person at the end of their life and a family member that has passed away in the last few hours that they had not even been informed of. Why? The family may not want to add to the distress of the sick person, or they may not be aware of it themselves.

There may be reports of the dying person talking to a discarnate individual that will give them the exact time and day when they will be collected and it has turned out to be so accurate you could set your watch by the information. Also they may reach their hands out upwards as if reaching for someone only then to lay down and pass away. It is as if the ethereal body is being pulled out from the physical body.

When I think about these occurrences I see in my minds-eye that person about to make their journey to spirit walking on a substantial wall between two properties. They can now see people on both sides of the garden wall and have conversations with whoever they wish on both sides, whilst we observe from one side missing out on the magnitude of the experience. Then, when they have walked the whole length of it which may take minutes, hours or even days they are merely helped down on the other side by those that also love them. We then see the person we know and love slowly slip away.

There are researchers that have studied this phenomenon and have refused to include patients in their statistics that have been sedated or heavily reliant on pain relief before their demise. Their results have shown that these patients still see and communicate with another dimension. Effectively, this then counteracts the reasons that will be explained by the medical profession, for behaviour close to physical death.

Making your pact

I wasn't at my father's bedside when he lost his battle with life. Rather than look for guilt within myself I have chosen to put it down to fate. He may have had weeks left but his health deteriorated rather quickly one night. I had started my new job, which was still within the probation period. Every time I did go to see him at the nursing home, in another county, he felt awkward about me coming all those miles to see him. He informed me that I should not have come because there was little I could do to help his plight. We were very similar people. He was very much a private man, who when he got sick, didn't really like people crowding around him.

I always left him by planting a kiss on his forehead. I reiterated one thing and that was if his pain ever got unbearable he was to ask God for help, not to think it, but it was to be said out loud. I also told him that it didn't matter if he believed or not (that God existed) because I knew that the higher power did not discriminate.

The thing I was thankful for, in hind sight, was that about two years before my father got sick I sat him down and told him that we needed to come up with a signal when one of us had died. My message for him was that the one that died should do anything they possibly could to annoy the other person's right ear. This could be a constant tickle, irritation, or a rattling of the ear drum just to show the other person that life was continuous.

I have never had ear complaints and can tell you that a few months after my father died my right ear (not my left) started to play up. My right eardrum goes haywire for few minutes at a time and then nothing, it's gone. It will then start again on another day. When this happens I try and greet my father like he has just entered the room.

It's all about having the confidence to do this with a person that means the world to you, even if you get a funny look. Keep talking to them and tell them what you would do and inform them what is expected of them. You may get similar results to me. Just like when his old mobile turns on without warning it always pulls at my heart strings as I know he is near.

Another time I believe he visits us is when our table makes a noise as if someone is trying to move it across the floor. In reflection, when he came to visit us in his later years we would both move the table together. This was when Samuel, dad and myself had our very own round robin table tennis tournament that we all loved. There was laughter and excitement as we entertained each other and agreed the winner stayed on the table for the next opponent. Samuel hated either of us making allowances for his age and would tell us "Don't go easy on me."

Chapter 24

Mick's family give me the nod

There is a part of us that seeks approval and recognition and I like to have mutual respect in place when I embark on something. I had always been in some form of contact with Mick's youngest sister called Sarah, who by coincidence happened to share the same name as Mick's girlfriend, so contacting her again wasn't going to be a problem.

We are all individuals, but I am always amazed by how different siblings can be from each other. However, in the case of Mick and his sister Sarah, there was always something of a spark that you could identify with even though they were two different souls. In many ways, they were like two peas in a pod. If you were a stranger and had walked into a crowded room seeing them both, at different times, and interacted with them you would want to take a step back look around and point at the other person and say, "What's the link?"

I had already relayed my shadow figure experience to Sarah when I had enough courage to explain the chain of events that happened. Although this was done over the telephone there was never an uncomfortable moment in the conversation between us. In fact Sarah, who is also open to the spirit world, had her own story to convey to me when I phoned her.

I had always wanted to tell Mick's mother and father about the event at my work that night but lacked the Dutch courage to do so, despite my efforts of putting myself forward for the eulogy at his funeral.

When something plays on your mind it continues to do so until you take action. I felt there could be a stumbling block if the book was to be finished. If I didn't have the approval that I wanted I felt like I would have to abort the mission at the eleventh hour. Therefore, every bead of sweat that had appeared on my brow and every tear that had welled up in my eyes; together with any words of wisdom that came out of me would now be futile if the events could not be brought up in their company.

My thoughts were if I had not offended Mick's family in the first six chapters or by showing them the introduction then I was not going to offend them with the rest of the book, after all, the truth is always the truth. So we got together in Sarah's front room on the 22nd June 2014. There was Mick's mother, father, sister, teenage Son, teenage nephew and brother-in-law together with Allison and myself.

When you strongly believe in the afterlife there is a part of you that feels like you represent a minority and as a consequence of this I felt I needed support. I had Allison beside me who could verify lots of phenomena and back-up the conversation I had with her on the morning of Friday the thirteenth (before the phone call came that told me to sit.) However, I needed a little extra to add to it so I showed them a collection of the high impact titles I had already read to calm my jittery nerves. Also, this was to show them that if these people had gone to such great lengths before me, then I shouldn't be as crazy as some of this was about to sound.

I hadn't seen Mick's parents since his funeral. We already had some cuddles and handshakes after we had stepped over the threshold. Then, I waited until I got the nod and started slowly. I told them if it seemed like I was going off at a tangent with my initial introduction and early chapters, to hold fast because it would all start to coincide. Mick's brother-in-law, Terry, who had also been in our class at secondary school (and previously played football with me for a local under 14's team) brought up the idea of one or two people reading to the whole room so we rolled with it.

As I said in a previous chapter, I have laid my soul bare writing this book and divulged information about my life that most would not want to tell their best friend. However, from my own perspective, I felt I had to because it gives the book the credence it deserves. My philosophy was, the more I talked with honesty, the more people would take the chain of events to their hearts and start observing their own immediate environment much more to see if they were also being watched over.

I looked around me as Terry and myself took it in turns to read to everyone. There were eyes welling up as well as tears falling from various quarters of the room as we went through the chapters. I looked down at one stage and saw my own hands trembling. Then a part of Mick's character would come out and just for a short time the tears would turn to laughter.

One of the most important things was to relive those memories of Mick in the book and give his children not only evidence that their own father was still watching over them but also for his children to have a friend's account of their father that they could hopefully cherish. When you have a memory that they don't it can give a different concept of the same person.

At the very end of this small get-together, I was seeing smiling faces and nods with words of genuine encouragement, just the result that I was seeking. I felt like I had got the reward both Mick and myself had wanted, the green light to proceed. My heart felt a leap of joy when Mick's son, called Kane, contacted me later and in a nutshell informed me that he was moved by what I had written and would be following things up by getting his own copy of the book.

Going back to the beginning of the book I conveyed that it should be about 'trust' before anything else. I was happy that particularly those in the room that had experience of my character for over two decades trusted the person they had known. With trust comes acceptance. In fact, Mick's dad revealed phenomenon that had happened to him since Mick passed.

The thing that I have learned from having an ADC involving Mick was that he had been given permission to come back and be noticed. Again, why me? Possibly because I was the most open to the world of spirit and also that this big day would come afterwards. I would be telling his family that he still existed and for them to know in their hearts that they would one day be reunited with him again.

Kind words from Sarah

The following touching words were received shortly after Mick's funeral in a thank you card. Although these words were deeply personal between two people I am sure you would agree that this book has been a deeply personal experience. I asked and was given permission to print these moving words from Sarah (Mick's girlfriend.)

28th October 2006

Dearest Grant,

Where do I begin with my thank you's? I can only imagine how you must be feeling at the moment, having lost your best friend of so many years. And it is difficult not to feel sad.

I feel as though I am so, so lucky to have loved and been loved by such a wonderful man and wish the accident had never happened. Everyone at Mick's funeral commented on your wonderful speech and I am sure Mick would have been so proud of you. Please take care and keep in touch.

Love to all

Sarah x

Chapter 25

Summing up
& signing out

This journey has always been about suppressing any ego that I may have had and listening. I have listened to the enlightened like a child listening to a parent in awe.

G.G.J.Sanders

When you engage in a conversation with someone you very often get an opinion. The current weather, the way the country is being run, the best holiday package to get, how the other person may dislike their job and much more. You may take that opinion and feel like you have got something from it or you may have wished that you hadn't started the conversation in the first place; it's all part of life.

If tomorrow, you asked your local vicar or someone that has a vast amount of medical knowledge about their views on the meaning of life and why living things suffer, you may get short or flippant answers in reply. Something like, "God works in mysterious ways" or "You live, it's unfair, you die and then that's it." My thoughts on these statements and I can assure you that they will come would be, 'shouldn't a person in your field be able to go on for hours about this?'

In this book, I have offered you my opinion. It is an opinion that weighs on proof that was given to me and my desire not to bury my head in the sand but look into it and it becoming a passion. It has been proven to me that around the time I breathe for the last time a transition occurs and another body (that will not be seen with the human eye) will rise out of my physical body and my soul survives. I may then be surrounded in darkness but soon see a pinpoint of light in the distance and I will be drawn to it because it represents my new home. I can then expect to be reunited not only with family and friends from this lifetime but other lifetimes too. I am indeed no different from anyone else reading this book.

I have tried (as best as I can) to tie-in as many subjects to give an idea of how things work. I have addressed near death experiences, out of body experiences, spirit guides, angels, cosmic ordering, hauntings, the afterlife, soul mates, choosing a life experience, reincarnation, vivid dreams, spirit communication, imaginary friends, advanced souls, things that happen under hypnosis, on people's death beds and so on.

One last scenario; picture a person going into a supermarket and buying a product that is sold in almost any other place. Then, they realise that there is something seriously wrong with it and although they don't have their receipt, they return to get their money back. They will, in all likelihood, be met with a gloomy face telling them that basically there is no proof that the product came from the store in question and it will automatically be handed back. They can get hot under the collar or calmly walk away but in reality they won't find anyone in this environment that will be willing to listen to an argument that is surrounded in absolute truth.

I realise metaphorically, I am the person returning to the store. I have had something happen to me and now I approach people and expect them to receive me on my terms. You can bet your bottom dollar that some people will be very uncomfortable with the information and scoff at it. I may even get called a loon. I can, like the person at the supermarket, get hot under the collar or say my piece and casually walk away.

When you analyse the supermarket experience or the paranormal experience the key factor here is simply the person receiving the story is either a listener (and can see the truth in your eyes) or they think you have no credibility and effectively cast you aside like a discarded cigarette.

One thing that I have learnt about the human personality is that because collectively we are the most powerful force on earth we can get carried away with our own greatness. If we look back on our own human history we have always thought that we are at the top of our game, because the cards we were holding at the time, felt like the best in the pack. The realisation is that when you look back and analyse the genius of our ways and understanding, the temple of cards we have constructed soon comes crashing down.

In recent times too we collectively think we are holding those great cards but only because we have nothing to compare ourselves to. In the next century, it may be asked why did previous generations produce vehicles that contaminated their immediate environment? Why did they have live power cables that were effectively exposed to the elements? Why did they have controls put in place to limit populations of species and ignore their own?

I can assure you that the vast amounts of UFO sightings around the planet are just as likely to be true as the story in my introduction that has been proven by science. I try and remember the phrase, 'just because it's not happening to you it doesn't mean that it's not happening.' This phrase can be related to almost anything.

Currently, by public debate, the jury still appears to be out as to whether we have even visited the moon. There have been songs written by music artists expressing their disbelief at people's plain acceptance of what they have seemingly been force fed.

I would say that alien life seems to be very interested in us and according to those that have experienced it with jaw-dropping technology at their disposal too. Why haven't these beings tried to attack us? Well, my answer would be that if we are governed by the akashic records, then why aren't they? They should be so spiritually advanced that they realise inflicting pain and hurt on others will ultimately come back to them which will lead them to have little desire to act in this way. You could also say that as there are vast numbers of other planets to inhabit, which has now been proven, why would they be interested in having ours?

In fact, it can make hairs on your body stand to attention when you read something in a book that was printed decades ago and then science effectively catches up and says the same thing, but only years after that book was published.

The future will create changes for us both good and bad but I am certain that the more we uncover and the more we get to understand, the nearer the spirit world will be drawn closer to our own reality. Who knows that in the next fifty years our technology will be so much more advanced that we can communicate clearly with the spirit world? When paranormal researchers pick up the odd word known as EVP's (electronic voice phenomenon) through their electrical devices this may be deemed as current as us trying to start a fire using flint.

In this book you will have picked up that I have a great respect for mediumship; it's true. However, it must be realised that mediums are like any other profession, where you will find different levels of ability. I have found through my education alone, that there are both wonderful teachers and those that perhaps, on reflection, should have chosen another profession.

Like one of my former English teachers. In the early days of secondary school, this teacher used to give us the same one hundred spellings every Friday. However, she never marked these papers or handed them back to us, showing us our mistakes, so we could actually learn from them. I have to assume our work went into the bin as soon as we left the classroom so she could get on with her weekend free of marking students work.

In essence, we didn't learn how to spell in these English lessons. So, I feel, when certain people give mediums a berating, they should not have this one size fits all one-dimensional approach. It's like me saying that all teachers are poor, it's simply untrue, and my ego would be involved if I made such a bizarre statement.

We live in a world where things are always becoming obsolete, so in fifty years will this be happening to our mediums of today? Will a device be created where it is like having your favourite discarnate relative on the phone for a chat? Personally, I will never rule this out even if it does not happen in this lifetime.

I reiterate that we are here to make our mistakes but where we show our character is when we learn from them and move on to pastures new, breaking the cycles of the past. I currently find the overused word 'proof' very frustrating for all the reasons that I have already mentioned. I have a similar relationship with the word 'perfect' because I truly understand that there is no such thing.

I believe that the souls that are learning all the things they need to are the ones that need to incarnate into this reality less and less. They have all learned very important lessons the school of life (earth) has been teaching them.

I also perceive that sheer materialism is counterproductive to the actual reasons we exist in this form. It is probably the biggest red herring of our existence. Imagine a soul continuing to come back to a physical life and trying desperately to create as much wealth as possible only to later realise that what they have been doing is a huge faux pas. Then, they must start again and again but what they have learnt from previous lives is withheld in the new life.

How many of these souls should we assume are currently involved in 'big business?' A high flying individual may have power and fortune burning brightly on the front gas whilst kindness and gratitude simmer gently on the back burner. I will leave this thought with you.

We are all here for lessons and some of these lessons are hard to take. They can be poverty, hardship, hunger, bullying, abuse, sickness, disease, neglect, abandonment, violence, racism, ridicule, coping with the death of loved ones (young and old) and much more. What if there is not one soul that will miss any one of these individual headings through time in the search for spiritual graduation?

When I think about reincarnation, I picture in my mind's eye a Girl Guide or Scout. They busy themselves by being put in new situations and try very hard to get their next badge. Lessons are being learnt until a full set has been achieved. When the full set is accomplished there is not much more left to strive towards and effectively we graduate. Through reincarnation, therefore, we obtain spiritual graduation. It's my view through immersing myself with information.

The way I view 'the Summerland' is we all have a mission (our daily lives) and when we come back from the mission (our contract with the divine) we largely get to live with paradise all around us until we agree the time may be right to make a return for the next mission. Our higher self, therefore, knowing what we are coming back to and what to expect; it seems we are prepared. We always appear to have a range of skills to cope for the environment we come back to. It's often just a case of unlocking the potential within ourselves.

Life can sometimes get topsy-turvy because we can chastise the ones that air their views and admit rather quickly that we don't like that person, whilst someone who may have stronger views keeps them withheld. We are then seemingly duped by the person who maintains the alternative approach because there are no views aired in public.

I have a warm admiration for people that have the conviction to say what others are merely thinking. For example, as a cricket fan, I strongly admire Geoffrey Boycott because he speaks his truth. He does this whether it is music to everybody's ears or not. His take on life represents my parenting style where I have always told my children what they need to hear, rather than what they want to hear. I believe that if we see no wrong in anything our children ever do and keep our views withheld then we have taught them next to nothing.

From my viewpoint, any love I have ever had for my children has not been geared towards what I can provide in terms of gifts. I didn't have to take them to Disney World to prove their best interests were always on my mind. I maintain that I have endeavoured to do all the things I could as a father with an undercurrent of kindness. Some people call the experience 'tough love.' It is with confidence I relate that my children will get to see this replay of events one day in its entirety (the life review.) We often don't understand our parents point of view until we actually become parents ourselves and go through similar life situations. Then things click into place.

Enjoy your life as much as you possibly can because it is a gift even though it doesn't always feel that way. I try and remember that all the bad things that have happened to me have merely happened to my physical body just with my soul pulling the strings. My physical body, that these things have happened to, will one day be left behind and my aim will be to leave the hurt behind with it. If I can't I may get offered a cleansing process in the spirit world.

As I sign out I would like to say use your gifts that you have been given, because we all have them, for greatness. Make a difference in any way you can. Make your life count. My soul feels true happiness when I offer my services to others, including vulnerable individuals that I have been lucky enough to perform in doing my day job, after realising I was on the wrong path. However, in all honesty, this new path could not have been found without a person on the old path offering me an olive branch to cling to.

My soul also feels happiness in offering you evidence of the continuation of life after the physical and I do hope this has been achieved within these pages.

Please remember that you are currently making the movie of your life, make your movie memorable and without regret of the things your true soul (your higher self) wanted to achieve. As souls, we have a fundamental responsibility to be kind to each other.

Acknowledgements

Firstly I would like to thank Mick Vaughan; a man that knows what friendship means on both sides of the veil. I would like to thank his family too for not only being the lovely individuals they are but having the confidence and belief in me with this book.

Next comes my wife. Allison, my future has always been in your eyes. We can talk about anything and everything and my most wonderful journeys in this life have been whilst by your side. Your advice is reflected within the pages of this book and I really have appreciated your keen brain. The idea of putting everything into words was your idea and then it became my passion. "Write a book, you can do it," I believe were your words.

Helen Watson (the lady with the kind eyes) thank you for offering to be the first person (outside my house) to read this book all the way through and in finding errors (my English is not perfect.) I would also like to thank Sue Hind because it has been a pleasure knowing you and learning from you (we never stop learning.)

Additional thanks go to all the people who as soon as they knew I was writing this book put their confidence in me by telling me they wanted a copy, you know who you are.

Last but not least, all my learning disability friends that I come into contact with on a daily basis. Thank you for your kindness, your smiles, laughter and attitudes towards life; it warms my soul and bounces off of me.

About the Author

During his life, the author has lived in Northamptonshire, the suburbs of London, Cambridgeshire and has now settled in Norfolk, living there for a considerable length of time. He met his wife Allison when they were teenagers. As a self-confessed family man, he is never happier than when he is with his wife, close family and pet dog as well as trying to enrich the lives of vulnerable individuals. He loves nature, soothing music, mixing with like-minded people and believes life is easier when you approach things with a smile and a sense of humour.

During the course of writing this book, the author and his wife have started fostering.

NOW TO BE MORE INFORMAL

If you have any comments or want to tell me your story that may have baffled your five senses (you will be surprised how many people have them) I can be contacted at ggjspiritual@hotmail.co.uk Please be mindful that if I never respond I may have taken my place in the world beyond.

Bibliography & Recommended Further Reading

Acorah, Derek, *The Psychic Adventures of Derek Acorah*, Llewellyn Publications, 2008

Alexander, (Dr) Eben, *Proof of Heaven: A Neurosurgeon's Journey into the Afterlife*, Piatkus, 2012

Alexander, Joseph, *Talking with Spirit*, Dunollie Ltd, 2004

Bowman, Carol, *Children's Past Lives: How Past Life Memories Affect Your Child*, Bantam Books, 1998

Brown, Robert, *We are Eternal: What the Spirits Tell me About Life After Death*, Warner Books, 2003

Byrne, Lorna, *Angels in my Hair*, Arrow Books, 2009

Callanan, Maggie, & Kelley, Patricia, *Final Gifts*, Simon & Schuster Inc, 2012

Cheung, Theresa, *The Afterlife is Real*, Simon & Schuster UK Ltd, 2013

Choquette, Sonia, *Diary of a Psychic: Shattering the Myths*, Hay House Inc, 2003

Cockell, Jenny, *Across Time & Death*, Simon & Schuster Inc/ Judy Piatkus Publishers Ltd, 1994

Davies, (Dr) Brenda, *Journey of the Soul*, Hodder & Stoughton, 2003

Dolan, Mia, *Haunted Homes: True Stories of Paranormal Investigations*, Harper Collins Publishers Ltd, 2006

Dolan, Mia, *The Gift*, Harper Collins Publishers Ltd, 2004

Donovan, Angela, *The Secrets of Psychic Success*, Rider, 2007

Edmonds, Noel, *Positively Happy: Cosmic Ways to Change Your Life*, Vermilion, 2007

Edward, John, *One Last Time*, Piatkus Books Ltd, 2012

Fenimore, Angie, *Beyond the Darkness*, Simon & Schuster Ltd, 1995

Findlay, Arthur, & Winkworth, Eileen, *More Truth*, Harmony Press Ltd, 1985

Findlay, Arthur, *On the Edge of the Etheric: Survival After Death Scientifically Explained,* PN Publishing, 2010

Flint, Leslie, *Voices in the Dark: My Life as a Medium*, Pembridge Publishing, 2007

Fry, Colin, *Secrets from the Afterlife*, Rider, 2008

Guggenheim, Bill, & Guggenheim, Judy, *Hello from Heaven,* Watkins Publishing, 2010

Heathcote-James, Emma, *After-death Communication*, Metro Publishing, 2008

Heathcote-James, Emma, *Seeing Angels*, John Blake Publishing Ltd, 2002

H.H. the Dalai Lama & Cutler, Howard, *The Art of Happiness*, Hodder Stoughton, 1999

Icke, David, *The Truth Vibrations*, Harper Collins, 1991

Jeffers, Susan, *End the Struggle & Dance with Life*, Hodder Stoughton, 2005

Jordan, Kathie, *The Birth Called Death*, Riverwood Books, 2010

Keane, Colm, *Going Home: Irish Stories from the Edge of Death*, Capel Island Press, 2009

Kessler, David, *Visions Trips & Crowded Rooms*, Hay House UK Ltd, 2010

Leininger, Bruce & Leininger, Andrea, *Soul Survivor: The Reincarnation of a World War II Fighter Pilot*, Hay House UK Ltd, 2009

Mc Mahon, Paddy, *There are no Goodbyes: Guided by Angels*, Harper Collins Publishers, 2011

Menet, Sarah, *There is no Death*, Mountain Top Publishing, 2003

Minns, Sue, *Soul Mates*, Hodder & Stoughton Ltd, 2005

Monroe, Robert, *Journeys out of the Body*, Souvenir Press, 2004

Moody, Raymond, *Life after Life*, Rider 2001

Newton, Michael, *Journey of Souls: Case Studies of Life between Lives*, Llewellyn, 2003

Playfair, Guy Lyon, *This House is Haunted*, White Crow Books, 2011

Richards, Stephen, *Cosmic Ordering Guide: Where Dreams can become Reality*, Mirage Publishing, 2006

Roache, William, *Soul on the Street*, Hay House UK Ltd, 2008

Sanders, Mary Anne, *Nearing Death Awareness*, Jessica Kingsley Publishers, 2007

Smedley, Jenny, *Soulmates*, Piatkus, 2013

Smith, Gordon, *Stories from the Other Side*, Hay House UK Ltd, 2006

Stockwell, Tony, *Embracing Eternity*, Hodder & Stoughton Ltd, 2007

Stokes, Doris, *Innocent Voices in my Ear*, MacDonald & Co Ltd, 1987

Stokes, Doris, *Whispering Voices*, MacDonald & Co Ltd, 1985

Stemman, Roy, *Reincarnation: True Stories of Past Lives*, Judy Piatkus Publishers Ltd, 1997

Swain, Jasper, *Heaven's Gift: Conversations beyond the Veil*, Kima Global Publishers, 1996

Tymn, Michael, *The Afterlife Revealed: What Happens After we Die*, White Crow Books, 2011

Williamson, Linda, *Ghosts and Earthbound Spirits*, Piatkus Books Ltd, 2006